KARMA

KARMA

◆

A YOGI'S GUIDE TO CRAFTING YOUR DESTINY

SADHGURU

HARMONY

BOOKS · NEW YORK

Library of Congress Cataloging-in-Publication Data
is available.

ISBN 978-0-593-23201-9
Ebook ISBN 978-0-593-23202-6

Printed in the United States of America

Book design by Andrea Lau
Jacket design by Anna Bauer Carr

10 9 8 7 6 5 4

First Edition

To all seekers . . .

The inner journey through an uncharted landscape can be
fraught with contradictions of thought, emotion, experience,
and action. This book strives to lift the haze of these
contradictions in the minds and hearts of all seekers of truth.

CONTENTS

◇◇◇

Unraveling Karma:
An Introduction

It happened.

On a certain day, Shankaran Pillai purchased a boat—a forty-foot ultra-luxurious yacht—for ten million dollars. He decided to take his new Puerto Rican bride out on the ocean for a romantic cruise.

On the way, misfortune struck. The yacht hit a rock and was wrecked.

As the brand-new boat sank into the ocean, Shankaran Pillai and his wife managed to extricate themselves. They swam for their lives and finally made their way to the shores of a nearby islet—a sandy sliver of land floating in the middle of nowhere, completely devoid of vegetation.

Shankaran Pillai and his wife had a few tins of canned food. They knew these would last them only a couple of days. They were in a fix.

Unperturbed, Shankaran Pillai settled down in a yogic

posture and assumed a serenely spiritual expression. His wife, however, was of a more volatile disposition.

"We're marooned!" she wept. "There's no human habitation in sight, no sign of any life here—no animals, no plants, nothing. What will we live on? How will we get out? What a terrible end to our dreams of marital bliss! What a terrible end to our lives!"

Shankaran Pillai continued to sit in his yogic posture, unruffled.

His wife was bewildered. "How can you sit like this? Don't you realize we're doomed? Can't you see we're going to die?"

Shankaran Pillai looked at her with calm compassion. "My dear, don't distress yourself," he said. "What I did not tell you before our wedding is that I have a history. I had previously availed myself of a student loan when I was studying in Tennessee. After my studies, I went to New York without repaying the loan. I was caught by my creditors three months later.

"But I managed to elude them and went away to California. There I got myself a car. Since I got myself a car loan, I said, why settle for a small car? I decided to get myself a Rolls-Royce with pure-gold trimmings, and I took a two-million-dollar loan to purchase the vehicle. Since I thought life would be somewhat difficult for me there, I took the car to Oregon.

"But they followed me there, too. After that episode, I took a home loan for five million dollars. I then happened to go to Mexico. But they followed me there six months later.

"After that, as you know, I married you and bought this yacht in Texas for ten million dollars. I haven't paid the first installment yet. So don't worry. Stay calm. Don't panic. They'll find us. They always do."

Shankaran Pillai's faith that he would be "found" (or more accurately, his realization that he could never escape his creditors!) is a phenomenon that the rest of the world knows by another name.

Karma.

The inescapable basis of our lives. The mechanism that decrees that we cannot evade the consequences of our own actions. The cycle that appears to follow us grimly and inexorably wherever we go.

Although the word is Indian in origin, *karma* is now a term that has invaded every dictionary. It is not merely the stuff of metaphysical tomes and academic treatises. It is instead a term that has pervaded lexicons across the world, from the esoteric to the pop.

How did this Sanskrit term enter every single language in the world? How do we account for its extraordinary popularity, its capacity to endure across the centuries?

There are many possible ways to explain this. But perhaps the primary explanation is just this: karma is the only concept in the world that addresses human perplexity in the face of suffering. It is the only logic that explains the seeming arbitrariness of the world we live in.

How else do we understand the pervasiveness of human anguish? How do we explain the horrors of war and terminal illness, the mute agony on the faces of starving children and traumatized prisoners? The unending catalog of savagery and conflict that has been the human experience for as long as we can remember?

Moreover, how do we answer these ancient questions: Why do terrible things happen to good people? Why does fortune so often favor those who seem cruel or unkind or the morally compromised? Why do life circumstances seem so random and capricious? Why does it feel sometimes that God—if one exists—must be playing marbles with the world? Why does the universe so often seem such a hostile, lawless, ungoverned place?

Perhaps no other word answers that bewildered human Why? as well as *karma* has.

Or can.

For far too long, the word has been either grotesquely over-simplified or needlessly mystified. It is time to explore the concept more deeply. It is time to unpack the most overused, abused, and yet indispensable word in the spiritual vocabulary of the world. It is time to examine how karma is connected to some of the most vital areas of human inquiry: the meaning of life and, above all, how to live it.

This book hopes to be both an exploration and a guide, offering the reader keys to living intelligently and joyfully in a challenging world. In the process, it seeks to restore the word *karma* to its original transformational potential. It hopes to peel off accretions of misunderstanding and look at karma in all its pristine power and with all its explosive resonance.

Throughout the book, I will outline a series of sutras to help you navigate the world of karma. *Sutra* literally means thread. Nobody wears a necklace for the sake of the thread, but without a thread there can be no necklace! In the yogic culture, a guru traditionally offered students a spare thread of guidance to navigate their way through life. But this volume hopes to provide readers both guidance and a detailed exposition of the subject of karma. It offers both pointers and the big picture—in other words, hopefully, both thread and necklace.

The book is divided into three parts. The first explores karma as a source of entanglement; the second explores the possibilities of freedom from this entanglement; and the third addresses frequent questions about the subject.

Part One examines the intricate workings of the karmic mechanism—one that is far more complex than most people realize. Part Two introduces the notion of karma yoga—ways to address and handle karma, as well as to liberate oneself from it. There is a pragmatic orientation to this section, but yoga is a science that cannot be imparted in its profundity by a book. It requires commitment and training under a spiritual master to be truly transformative. A book can, however, illuminate and inspire a potential path, and this is what this section hopes to do.

A word of caution: You may find, as you journey deeper into this book, that you encounter various technical terms. But don't lose heart. Karma is not a poetic subject. It is a complex domain—one that involves precise, even clinical, concepts and distinctions. Yet neither is karma a sterile theme. It is the basis of human existence—a life-and-death issue, in fact. There can be nothing narrowly academic about such a discussion.

Several chapters in Parts One and Two are interspersed with sections called sadhanas. In Sanskrit, *sadhana* means a device or tool. These tools offer you an opportunity to put into practice some of the insights you encounter in each chapter and to test them in the laboratory of your experience.

Part Three is devoted to questions. These are searching, heartfelt questions. Questions that I have been asked in programs and conversations over three and a half decades. Questions that recur simply because human curiosity about karma is lingering, persistent, frequently urgent. The confusion about this subject is genuine, the longing for clarity equally authentic.

Perhaps some of these questions will resonate with you. Others may actually sound like your very own questions. Very few questions, since the dawn of time, have been truly new. The contexts and specifics may change, but the need to make sense of a world of pain and injustice continues to stay relevant, while the human thirst to fathom the mysteries of life will endure until the end of time.

Let us unravel karma.

PART ONE

◆

PART FIVE

◇◇◇

A Note to the Reader

The word *sadhguru*, as I often point out, means an uneducated guru. An uneducated guru does not come from accumulated scriptural information, but from a moment-to-moment inner knowing. I come, therefore, from a place of direct experience, not secondhand knowledge.

My approach to karma, therefore, is not—and has never been—that of a scholar. When I speak of karma, I am not drawing on doctrine. I am drawing on perception. Conceptual knowledge is the way of the academic. Perceptual knowing is the way of the yogi.

Part One of this book explains karma—in all its complexity and multidimensionality. It may seem to deal with pure concepts, sometimes challenging ones. But I want to emphasize that these are not abstruse theories but, rather, direct insights into the actual workings of karma.

This is a section for the thirsty. It is for those who have nursed questions over the years, questions such as What is karma?

How does it accumulate? What makes the machinery work? When did this whole complicated and crazy cycle begin? It is for those who aren't looking for mere user manuals, but for a glimpse into the very mechanism of the karmic wheel.

This section examines how the wheel comes into being and gains momentum. It leads you step by step into the subject of karma—what it is; how it accumulates; the many ways in which human personality is shaped; the incredibly vast reservoir of memory that every individual carries; the role of volition; the subtle ways in which karma adheres to us even when we seek to free ourselves of it.

Spiritual seekers usually want to shed their karma, but it is important to remember that karma is *not* our enemy. It is not necessary to eliminate all karma to lead a life of well-being. Indeed, we would not be able to live without karma, for human life is sustained by it. At the same time, karma can become wounding and deeply entangling if we do not learn how to handle it.

The yogic system gives no commandments whatsoever. It leaves you free to choose whether you want to generate positive karma for the future, distance yourself from your karmic package, or dissolve it altogether. Even as this book explores and outlines these various possibilities, the choice is yours.

If you find your foot recurrently crushed under a wheel, the problem is not with the wheel. The problem is that you have no clue how to ride it. The aim of this book is not to reinvent the wheel but to suggest ways to ride it joyfully toward the destination of your choice, secure in the knowledge that you are in control of your own journey.

ONE

Karma: The Eternal Enigma

SUTRA #1

*Karma is about becoming the source of one's own creation.
In shifting responsibility from heaven to oneself,
one becomes the very maker of one's destiny.*

In the Driver's Seat

It happened.

Once the pope went to the United States. His schedule was a busy one, with engagements in various cities. One day, he happened to be in Louisiana in a chauffeur-driven stretch limo—the vehicle that demonstrates the quintessentially American ability to stretch a limousine to its limits.

The pope was excited because he had never driven a car like this. He told the chauffeur, "I would like to drive."

How could the chauffeur refuse the pope? He said, "Of course, Holy Father."

So the pope took the wheel and the chauffeur took the back-seat. The pope started enjoying the car and his foot got heavy on the gas pedal. He hit ninety and then a hundred miles an hour. He did not realize how fast he was going.

Now, the Louisiana police, known to be sticklers when it comes to speed breaking, swung into action. When the pope in the zooming limo saw the flashing light behind him, he pulled over to the shoulder of the road.

The cop got out and, carefully, with his hand on his gun, slowly approached the car. He looked in. He saw it was the pope himself driving! He peered into the back seat and saw somebody else sitting there.

"Wait," he said.

He went back to his car, took out the radio, and called the police chief. He said, "Captain, I've got a real big fish."

"Oh, come on. Who is it? Bonnie and Clyde?"

"No, somebody much bigger than that."

"Sweet Jesus, have you got Al Capone?"

"Oh no, somebody much, much bigger."

"What, you think you've got the president of the United States of America himself?"

"No, somebody far bigger than that!"

"Come on, who the hell can be bigger than the president of the United States? What have you got on your hands?"

The cop replied, "I don't know, but he's got the pope as his chauffeur!"

And that brings us to the crux of the matter: most people don't have a clue who is driving their car!

Look around you. Ask yourself how many people you know are living with any real understanding of the crazy locomotive called life. Most people are passive pawns in the ride, clueless about how the machinery works, the source of its octane, how to manage its direction or its velocity, or, above all, who their chauffeur is. They talk of free will, liberty, and independence. But they have little or no control over their lives. Their destiny is something they create unconsciously.

Welcome to karma, a dimension that puts you squarely back where you belong, where you were meant to belong all along: in the driver's seat.

Demystifying Karma

With that we come to the central question of this book: What *is* karma?

Literally, the word means action.

Unfortunately, most people have understood action in terms of good and bad deeds. They see karma as a balance sheet of merits and demerits, virtues and sins. A life audit of sorts. To others, it is a ledger maintained by some divine chartered accountant who assigns some people to celestial bliss and consigns others to a nether world or into the maw of some recycling machine that spews them back into this world to suffer some more.

This is not merely false and absurd. It is tragic.

This notion has created generations of puzzled and fearful human beings who use the term indiscriminately, without a clue of what it means. It has spawned a brand of fatalism that has paralyzed vast segments of people and has been used to validate social injustices and political tyrannies of various kinds. It has also led to much spurious philosophizing and empty academic debate and has, of course, boosted the fortune-telling industry!

Let us shatter the first myth.

In actual fact, karma has *nothing* to do with reward and punishment. It has nothing to do with some despotic life auditor up in the sky, working with primitive devices of carrot and stick. It has nothing to do with a benign god up in the heavens. Nothing to do with divine retribution. Nothing to do with virtue and sin, good and evil, God and Mr. Lucifer.

Karma simply means we have created the blueprint for our lives. It means we are the makers of our own fate. When we say "This is my karma," we are actually saying "I am responsible for my life."

Karma is about becoming the source of one's own creation. In shifting responsibility from heaven to oneself, one becomes the very maker of one's destiny.

Karma is the natural basis of all existence. It is not a law that is imposed from above. It does not allow us to outsource our responsibility anywhere else; it does not allow us to blame our parents, our teachers, our countries, our politicians, our gods, or our fates. It makes each one of us squarely responsible for our own destinies and, above all, the nature of our experience of life.

So the only relevant question here is, Are you *ready* for karma?

Are you ready to hear about a dimension that is so empowering that it tells you that you are fully capable of taking the reins of your life into your own hands?

If not, read no further.

If you are willing, and if you are curious to find out more about how this mechanism works, this book could be your key. All you need to do after this is to fire up your engine and set off on your new life journey. Once you are at the wheel, your experience of the ride will never be the same again.

It is important to remember one thing, however. Karma is not a doctrine. You do not get any brownie points for subscribing to it. You do not get any negative marks for disbelieving it. Karma is not a creed, a scripture, an ideology, a philosophy, or a theory. It is simply the way things are. It is an existential mechanism. Like the sun, it operates whether you acknowledge it or not, whether you pay obeisance to it or ignore it. It is not looking for a fan club.

It simply turns you from a white-knuckled, terror-struck passenger in the backseat into a confident driver, in charge of the wheel, joyfully navigating the course of your own destiny.

The Karmic Cycle

To turn driver instead of passenger, however, you need to start by knowing a few basic rules about how the karmic mechanism works.

Let us start by addressing a fundamental misunderstanding. Although karma means action, it does not necessarily refer to *physical* deeds. It does not necessarily refer to what you do in the outside world—whether it be acts of charity or acts of villainy.

Instead, karma is action on three levels: *body, mind,* and *energy.* Whatever you do on these three levels leaves a certain residue or imprint upon you.

What does this mean?

It is quite simple. Your five senses are collecting data from the outside world every moment of your life. You are literally being bombarded with stimuli at every instant. Over time, this enormous volume of sense impressions begins to assume a certain distinctive pattern within you. This pattern slowly shapes itself into behavioral tendencies. A cluster of tendencies hardens over time into what you call your personality, or what you claim to be your true nature.

It works in the reverse as well: Your mind shapes the way you experience the world around you. This becomes your karma—an orientation to life that you have created for yourself in relative unawareness. You are not aware of how these tendencies develop.

But what you consider to be "myself" is just an accumulation of habits, predispositions, and tendencies you have acquired over time without being conscious of the process.

Take a simple example. Some people may have been joyful children but are now unhappy adults. There may have been life events that triggered that unhappiness. But in most cases, people have no clue how and when they acquired this persona. If they had created their personality consciously, they would have crafted themselves quite differently. But somewhere along the way, by following the diktats of their unexamined reactions and tendencies, chronic unhappiness became their defining characteristic.

In other words, karma is like old software that you have written for yourself *unconsciously*.

And, of course, you're updating it on a daily basis!

Depending on the type of physical, mental, and energetic actions you perform, you write your software. Once that software is written, your whole system functions accordingly. Based on the information from the past, certain memory patterns keep recurring. Now your life turns habitual, repetitive, and cyclical. Over time, you become ensnared by your patterns. Like so many people, you probably don't know why certain situations keep recurring in your inner and outer life. This is because these patterns are unconscious. As time goes on, you turn into a puppet of your accumulated past.

The lives of many people, for instance, are dominated by food or substance abuse. Chemical addiction certainly plays a role here, but the primary problem is that they have set up a recurrent pattern in their life. However hard they try to emerge from it, they keep falling back into the trap. If one does not consciously rewrite one's karmic software, the regularity of the pattern can feel like it is being imposed from without, rather than initiated from within. But this software is not a fate to be endured. It *can* be rewritten, dropped, or distanced, as we will see later in this book.

The karmic mechanism is ceaseless. Every mental fluctuation in you creates a chemical reaction, which then proceeds to provoke a physical sensation. This sensation, in turn, reinforces the chemical reaction, which then strengthens the mental fluctuation. Over time, your very chemistry is determined by a series of unconscious reactions to sensory and mental stimuli.

Now, if you simply think about something that excites you, you can actually feel certain sensations in your body. This can be empirically verified. We now know that the human being is a psychosomatic organism—that whatever happens in the mind immediately imprints itself on the body as a chemical process. If you think of mountains, for instance, your chemistry will react in one way; if you think of tigers, it reacts in another. So for every minute mental fluctuation, there is a certain type of chemical reaction and sensation. You may not even be aware of it unless the sensations become acute. All these sensations register and over time become the blueprint of your unconscious mind. You are therefore a living repository of karmic memory on levels you are not aware of.

Today, research has shown that psychological and emotional traumas can contribute to your risk for mental and physical health problems. We are told that mental distress can lead to cardiac problems. None of this is new. People always knew that if you go through psychological upheavals, your heart will break! All this happens because your body chemistry changes over a period of time as a result of constant mental and emotional fluctuation.

This is a vicious cycle. If you touch the firmament of your mind just once, the resulting ripples are enough to keep going for lifetimes. The mind is a process that picks up momentum without any assistance from you. You may have noticed that when you were eighteen, you were generally able to shrug off difficulties and move on. That ability was more challenged by thirty. By forty-five, many things seemed to bother you. And, by sixty, you find it almost impossible to pick yourself up, adapt, and move on.

This mentality is pervasive—you can see it all around you. At eighteen, people are often anxious about their future. At seventy, when most of their life is behind them, they are still worried! They have become such veterans at the business that they worry for no reason at all. This is because the cycle from mental fluctuation to chemical reaction to sensation (which then, in turn, produces a chemical reaction that leads again to a mental fluctuation) has gathered momentum. Over time, this has a cumulative impact on cellular and genetic memory, as well as on the energy system.

The unconscious mind is therefore a tremendous library of karmic memory. You would find this information very useful if you were approaching it consciously. The problem is that it manifests all the time, without your permission! You feel like one big mess because you are punching your psychological keyboard randomly all the time.

Think of a CD on which music is recorded. The disk is like your body—whether physical, mental, or energetic. The music is analogous to the impression recorded upon your body. Now, the music is just a small impression on a compact disk. But when you play the CD, you do not experience the disk; you experience the music. Karma is similar. You are not actively experiencing your energetic or mental or physical body. You are only facing the music! And you cannot stop it. You are experiencing your karmic impressions and imprints all the time. And you cannot bring these to a halt.

The Tedium and Tyranny of Karma

The level at which the compulsiveness of karma operates may surprise you. When you walk into an auditorium or conference room, the seat you choose may seem like a decision you made freely. But often a level of karmic compulsion is involved. If you attend the same conference or class for the next five days, you may notice that you are likely to sit in the same place each day.

Many years ago, when I was training teachers to impart my Inner Engineering program in different places, the new trainee teachers would often ask, "Sadhguru, what kind of questions are students likely to ask? What can we expect and how do we deal with it?" So I made a chart for them of the arrangement of the class and told them, "See, if a person comes and settles down *here,* this is the kind of question they are going to ask. If a participant settles down *there,* that is what they are going to ask." Now, of course, there were exceptions: a latecomer might choose a place based only on the seat that is available. But ninety percent of the time it happened exactly the way I said it would! That is how predictable karma is.

So karma is *not some external system of crime and punishment.* It is an internal cycle generated by you. These patterns are not oppressing you from without, but from *within.* Externally, it may be a new day. You may have a new job, a new home, a new life partner, a new baby. You may even be in a new country. But, internally, you are experiencing the same cycles—the same internal oscillations, the same behavioral shifts, the same mental reactions, the same psychological tendencies.

Everything has changed except for your experience. You can keep modifying the outer environment, but nothing will work because you haven't figured out how to change *your karma*. Something else seems to be pushing your buttons. Someone else seems to be driving your car.

For every other creature on this planet, the struggles are essentially physical. If they eat well, they are just fine. But human beings are different. For humans, when the stomach is empty, there is only one problem; but when the stomach is full, there are one hundred problems! You may talk freedom, but you are gold-plating your limitations all the time in absolute unawareness. Even as you extol the values of independence, everything about you—not just the way you look or feel or think, but even the way you sit or stand or walk—is determined by your past patterns.

Do not forget that in addition to being unconscious and compulsive, karma is also deeply cyclical. The karmic information within your system is encoded in different kinds of cycles. The largest cycle is the solar cycle, because everything—animate and inanimate—in this solar system is deeply influenced by the sun. Our planet is no exception. The solar cycle is a period of 4,356 days (nearly 12 years). Someone who lives according to the solar cycle leads a life of great health, well-being, alignment, and minimal friction.

As the length of a karmic cycle decreases, life becomes progressively more unbalanced. If your life runs in three- or six-month cycles, you are in a serious state of psychological imbalance. The same inner upheavals or life situations will keep recurring every few months. If your life is determined by a twenty-eight-day cycle—the lunar cycle, which is also the shortest one—you could well be considered deranged or psychotic. The word *loony*, as you know, is linked to the word *lunar*, and this is no coincidence. It should be remembered, however, that the karmic cycle has nothing to do with the reproductive cycles of the female body.

Now, if we do not break these internal and external patterns, nothing new will ever happen. You might have noticed that the more successful you become, the more frustrated you get, because somewhere unconsciously you sense that you are simply going around in circles. You may have learned to ride the cycle, but you are not free from it.

With yogic practices, the aspiration is to move toward the solar cycle so your balance and stability are assured. You may not be able to change your past action and the mental and emotional karma you accumulated, but you no longer slide into short-spin cycles. You no longer wear your karma as a skin-tight garment; you learn to wear it loosely. You hold it at a distance.

The problem is that people do not realize just how tenacious karma is. You could meet with an accident and die, but your karma is not destroyed. You could break your head and blow all your brains out, but the karma continues! That is how resilient, how relentless, how subtle the karmic mechanism is. And that is why freedom from the cycle so often seems like such a remote possibility.

The yogic tradition tells us that in addition to the physical body (the *annamayakosha*), each human being has a mental body (*manomayakosha*) and an energy body (*pranamayakosha*). There are subtler bodies as well, known as the etheric body (*vignanamayakosha*) and the bliss body (*anandamayakosha*). But the accumulation of karma essentially happens on the levels of the first three bodies: physical, mental, and energetic.

Therefore, even if you break your body and your mind, your life energy continues to bear the karmic imprint, like a computer hard disk. The backup systems are so efficient that even if you lose your body or your mind, you still do not lose your karma.

However, it does not matter what volumes of karma you have, the moment you start stepping into the subtler dimensions of the etheric and bliss bodies, your karma cannot touch you. The law of cause and effect can operate only on the physical, mental, and energy levels. Beyond that, it has no impact. The moment you begin to taste the divine, as it were, your karma has no hold over you. (We will explore this at greater length in Part Two of this book.)

There was a time when human beings wrote on stone tablets. From stone tablets we moved to leaves, and then we came to books. From books we moved to cassettes and CDs. We have now come to the age of the microchip. What could be stored on a million stone tablets is encrypted in the tiniest speck imaginable. It won't be long before technology finds a way to start recording information on pure energy itself. This may not yet have manifested in modern technology, but eventually it will happen. I say this not out of any technological knowledge but because I know how the inner mechanism works. And the atomic and the cosmic, the individual and the universal, mirror each other on every level.

Right now the same electricity that powers your lightbulb becomes light; the same electricity that powers your air conditioner makes the air cool; the same electricity that powers a microphone becomes amplified sound. This is not because the electricity is intelligent. It is simply the mechanism of the appliance. But a day will come when we will have "smart electricity." We will be able to load memory onto the energy of electricity directly so the very electric stream can come with an intent. It will have the information to behave in specific ways and to make certain decisions. Maybe the day is still far away, but I have no doubt we are heading there.

When I initiate groups of people into a spiritual process,

each person's energies behave differently, depending upon their karmic information. Though the same process is offered to everybody, each person's energy response depends upon the type of karma they carry. The energy body responds according to the kind of software imprinted upon it. That is why two people's response to an initiation is never the same.

In short, karma operates on many different planes. You cannot shake it off with physical illness or accident, dementia, psychosis, or death. You will notice that even those who are mentally ill do not behave similarly. Their karmic structure may be out of control, but it still governs the way they behave. Unless you loosen the grip of karma, there is no way out.

This is the deadly tedium and tyranny of the karmic rut.

This is also why people have from time immemorial sought something more—even though they do not know what it is. This condition has been given many names: from existential discontent and ennui to simple anxiety and unease. It is the sense of not living life at full throttle, not understanding its purpose, its beginning or its end, its direction or the source of its propulsion. It is the age-old human resentment of powerlessness, of limitation.

The Smell of Bondage

As we have seen, whatever you do with your body, mind, or energy leaves a certain imprint. These imprints configure themselves into tendencies. These tendencies have been traditionally described in India by a wonderfully apt word: *vasana*. Literally, *vasana* means *smell*. This "smell" is generated by a vast accumulation of impressions caused by your physical, mental, emotional, and energy actions. Depending upon the type of smell you emit, you attract certain kinds of life situations to yourself.

Think of a flower. A flower has a certain kind of vasana. It is this fragrance that draws certain kinds of life to it. It cannot move and it has no volition, but because of its fragrance, it may be chosen for worship in a temple sanctum. In fact, thanks to its vasana, it gains entry where few human beings are permitted.

It is not so different for human beings. Here the word *smell* does not imply an odor. There is no value judgment attached to the word. It simply means that if you exude a particular kind of vasana, existence will ensure you land up in certain places at certain times. If you exude another type of vasana, existence will make sure you land up in certain other places. So what moves toward you and also what moves away from you are determined by the smell that emanates from you. Your vasana depends, of course, entirely on the kind of residual memory or karmic content you carry.

This works in subtle ways. You may not be aware of it, but in wakefulness and sleep, you are performing karma. A simple thought pattern could make you function in specific ways. If you keep thinking about the movies, or perhaps a particular movie star, for instance, you are very likely to see a particular person in a crowd who shares your passion. You might miss the others: those who love books, or meditation, or something else. If you see a thousand faces before you, your vasana is likely to draw you toward someone who is similarly inclined.

It happened.

At a certain point as a teenager, I got myself a huge cobra—a marvelous twelve-foot-long specimen. It had made its way into a local tube-light factory, and I caught it, much to the relief of the factory workers. I hid it under my bed in a large glass container. Somehow, one day it managed to escape.

When my father heard a loud hiss from my room, he went down on his knees to find out what the matter was. When he saw the cobra, he absolutely freaked out. He ran out of the room crying "Cobra, cobra!" When I entered the scene, everyone at home was literally standing on chairs and sofas. On the other hand, I ran into the room to protect my snake, anxious that my companion would be thrown out! My parents' vasana produced aversion; my vasana produced attraction.

I managed to smuggle the same snake back and housed it later on the rooftop of my home in a large cage. On another occasion, it managed to escape again. I happened to be out at the time. As I came riding back on my bicycle, I saw my parents standing outside the house, consternation written large upon their faces. The school adjacent to the house had just let up at four in the afternoon. A huge crowd had gathered around the snake. Everyone was terrified. As I drew close, I realized what was going on. I knew I could not go home. There would be too much drama. I simply zoomed by, scooped up my cobra by the middle with one hand, and rode away!

This story exemplifies vasanas at work. What provoked terror for my parents and others produced a very different response in me. I have never felt any aversion to snakes. My sense of kinship with them is an ancient vasana that I carry. I have always been comfortable around these exotic creatures. Ever since childhood, I have been able to intuitively track their presence in the wild. If I simply followed my sense of smell, I would know under exactly which rock the snake could be found. I developed quite a reputation in my neighborhood as a snake catcher.

There are many reasons for my attraction to snakes. The connection between yogis and snakes is an old one. Both exude a vasana that draws them to each other. The snake is an incredibly perceptive creature and is instinctively drawn to higher levels of energy. This is why Adiyogi (Shiva), the first yogi, is always depicted in traditional iconography with a snake around his throat.

In all those cultures in which people have delved into extrasensory perception, the snake plays a pivotal role. The traditional veneration of snakes, cows, and crows in India is based on the awareness that these creatures represent an advanced stage of existential development.

Since yogis constantly aspire to enhance their perception, the snake is a particularly important presence in the yogic tradition. The cobra is revered as the only creature that can perceive the subtle etheric dimension, even in the daytime. Not surprisingly, it plays a significant role in several creation myths as well, even if it has sometimes been disparaged by those who feared its capabilities.

Yet another reason for this vasana is the connection between the snake and the kundalini, the coiled energy that lies at the base of the human spine (which yoga consciously harnesses for spiritual development). The kundalini energy has been described as "serpent energy" because of its similarity to the snake in terms of a shared pattern of movement and stillness.

In the early days of my work as a guru, when I wanted to consecrate a powerful energy form called the Dhyanalinga (a unique structure in which all seven chakras, or energy centers, are operating at their optimal capacity), I needed to draw very fierce and intense disciples around me to assist with this project. Now that this mission is complete, I have altered my vasana completely. Because the need for that kind of concentrated energy work is over, I draw other kinds of people to me. I am probably unrecognizable to the people who knew me then, because I *am* a different person. Depending on the nature of the work, I adjust the tone of my vasana. This may be puzzling to some. But this is the way every spiritual master operates.

However, the capacity to adjust one's vasana is not an option reserved only for the spiritually adept. It is possible for each individual to choose not to be a victim of their vasana to a great extent. All it takes is a certain awareness. With a little awareness, every human being can begin to transform habit into choice, compulsion into consciousness.

It is important to see that whatever seems determined in your life has been determined by you unconsciously. You have written your own software. Depending on the way you have written your software, that is the way you think, that is the way you feel, that is the way you act, and that is what you invite into your life. Depending on the kind of "fragrance" you emit, you attract life situations. Some people seem to constantly attract pleasant situations; others seem to constantly attract unpleasant ones. Or perhaps you see this in different phases in your life. In some phases, wonderful things seem to keep happening; in others, adverse circumstances keep recurring. Now, this simply depends on what you have in your karmic reservoir. Today you have rotten fish, so you attract some terrible situations; tomorrow you have flowers, so you attract better situations. One thing that we are trying to change through yoga (and hopefully, this book) is the kind of fragrance you throw out into the world.

Many people talk freedom but they secretly fear it. They feel secure in bondage. Other people opt for bondage because identification with an ideology, a religion, a relationship, or even a gadget enhances their identity in some way. Consider something as simple as your cell phone. If it is used to enhance activity, it can be a source of empowerment. But if it is used to enhance identity, it becomes a source of bondage. In this way, people acquire vasanas unconsciously, often believing they are choosing freedom when they are actually choosing enslavement.

It happened.

Some years ago, when conducting a yoga program in southern India, I stayed in a village called Velayudhampalayam. My lodging was opposite a hill. I was told that Jain monks had lived and meditated in these hill caves more than nineteen hundred years ago. This antiquity piqued my interest, because it meant these monks had lived only a few centuries after the great Jain teacher and guru Mahavira.

One afternoon, I climbed up, with a few volunteers, to a beautiful cave located like a bird's perch in the rocks. The inside was filthy, strewn with bottles and graffiti. In India, every second rock and monument has the initials of tourists and visiting lovers scrawled upon it. These caves were no different; they were liberally scratched with the usual "KPT loves SRM" type of stuff. So we cleaned up the place.

Now, there were rough indentations in the rock floor, which clearly served as beds for the monks. I sat down on one of these beds. I suddenly found my body beginning to pulsate powerfully. Intrigued, I decided to spend the night there.

It was a night of revelation. I realized that the subtle body of the monk who had been there centuries ago was still incredibly alive. I could tell, for instance, that he had no left leg; it had been amputated just below the knee.

Now, these monks led quiet, isolated lives and had done nothing of consequence in the outside world. But they had left behind such a profound imprint that I could tell everything about their lives and their spiritual practices. The great rulers of those times are more or less forgotten. The richest folk and the most learned men and women of those times are erased from our memory. But these simple monks are as alive today as they were nineteen hundred years ago! Their stories are available to those who are receptive, and they are capable of inspiring us to this very day. This is the nature of the right kind of inner energy work. It is imperishable.

Every individual's energies carry a certain fragrance. The

physical body falls back to the Earth; however, the residue of each one of our thoughts, actions, and, above all, our energies lingers on. This imprint can last for millennia after our time. The more conscious the energy work, the more enduring it is.

It is up to us to decide the nature of our bequest to the planet. This is what the anonymous Jain monks of Velayudhampalayam did. Aware that every action has a consequence, they chose to live consciously. As a result, they achieved a certain kind of immortality that the rich and powerful in the history of the world have seldom managed to attain.

SADHANA

A simple way to become aware of your vasana is to try to stay away for a length of time from that which you like, long for, love, or consider to be most precious. The intensity of the pangs you go through when you stay away tells you something about the nature and depth of your vasana.

Now that you have identified your vasana, you can start working on transformation. If you think your entanglement is related to food, wait a few moments before you have a meal. If you are eagerly awaiting the arrival of a loved one, consciously wait a few moments longer before you meet them. Depending on how deeply entangled you think you are, wait consciously for a few more moments before you engage in that activity or interaction. You will see that your experience of food or love or life generally becomes that much more profound. Gradually, the two minutes of waiting for a meal could be extended for two hours or for an entire day. This deceptively simple exercise can mark the beginning of a tremendous inner shift.

Consciousness is not a matter of behavior. It is the nature of existence. Compulsiveness, however, is behavioral. The moment you wait before you engage in a compulsion, you are aligning yourself with the conscious nature of existence. Over time, this helps weaken the compulsive nature of your behavior.

TWO

Volition: The Basis of Karma

SUTRA #2

Ultimately, life is neither suffering nor bliss.
It is what you make it.

The Consequence of Calculation

It happened.

On a certain evening, two friends were walking together. It was their weekly custom to visit a prostitute every Saturday evening. While they were walking toward the prostitute's house, they heard a voice delivering a discourse on the Bhagavad Gita, India's great sacred text.

One friend was seized by guilt. He decided not to visit the prostitute and said he would rather improve himself by attending the lecture on the Gita. The other man left him there and went ahead.

Now, the man sitting in the lecture hall found his thoughts

were full of his friend who was with the prostitute. He began to envy him. While he was stuck in this lecture room, the other man, he was convinced, was having the time of his life. He couldn't help feeling his friend was far more intelligent in choosing the brothel over a scriptural discourse.

Now, the man who had gone to the prostitute's house found his mind was full of his friend at the lecture hall. He was filled with admiration for his friend who had chosen the path to liberation by opting for a spiritual discourse over carnal pleasures.

This story was often related by the great twentieth-century Indian mystic Sri Ramakrishna Paramahamsa. He always drew attention to the central paradox: it is the man at the Gita discourse (who kept thinking about what was happening in the prostitute's house) who piled up the adverse karma. It is he who suffered, Sri Ramakrishna pointed out, much more than the man who visited the prostitute.

Why?

Because although karma denotes action of body, mind, and energy, it is *not* about action alone. The man who went to the prostitute did not pile up as much karma as his friend because *he did not make a calculation.* His friend, on the other hand, secretly wished he was with her but believed that by going to the discourse he would get one step closer to heaven. That calculation meant an acquisition of more karma. Ironically, the man who thought about how to shed karma actually ended up accumulating it!

The man with the prostitute, on the other hand, was seized by a sense of the limitation of his experience. That would have impelled him in the future to seek something more. So the experience with the prostitute became a trigger for his personal growth.

This story points to a common mistake. People often assume

karma is only about external action. They think performing acts of charity and virtue will earn them good karma. What they never quite realize is that it is about something much subtler.

Karma is much more fundamentally about *volition*.

The reason why religious teachings all over the world are always talking about love is that the moment you become loving, you are naturally at your best in relation to others. The moment you view everyone with love, your intention is automatically inclusive. Regardless of what blunders you may commit in the name of love, the karma still does not accumulate beyond a point.

Your intention makes all the difference. If you say something prompted by love, and another person gets hurt, that is his karma, not yours. But if you say something out of hatred and another person has no problem with it, it is good karma for them and not for you! You still acquire negative karma. How the recipient of your hatred reacts is not the point. The accumulation of karma is determined by your intention, not merely by its impact on someone else.

Consider another situation. Let us say you are playing with a knife. It accidentally hits someone and they fall down dead. This is one kind of karma. In another scenario, you get into an argument with someone while cutting vegetables. In the heat of the moment, you stab them and they die. In a third situation, you meticulously plan how you would dispose of an enemy; you pursue them and thrust a knife into them. In a fourth scenario, you behave in a very friendly manner with someone and invite them over to dinner; after a wonderfully cordial meal, when they are sitting back satiated, you slit their throat. This is yet another kind of karma. In a fifth situation, you are perfectly normal in your behavior with a person, but internally you keep plotting all the terrible things you want to do to them.

In the first four cases, the same ingredients are present: you, the other person, the knife, and death. The karma, however, is not the same. It is not difficult to guess which will breed the worst karmas. By *worst*, I do not mean the most immoral; I mean that which creates the worst consequences for you. The consequence for the other person is the same, but the impact on you is determined by the nature of your volition. It is the level of bitterness and hatred that causes karma, not the act alone.

The fifth scenario is actually the worst in terms of karmic accumulation. The first four talk about situations in which the result is the same for the other person. In the fifth, there is no consequence for the other person. They have been released from their karma, so it is good for them. But your karma is much stronger because, here, you are repeating the act a million times within yourself. Acting out the bitterness externally has a grave physical consequence for you (a jail sentence). But allowing the bitterness to grow and multiply within has even deeper internal consequences. Intention motivated by a personal agenda always accrues much more karma. If you keep repeating the same mental action, it is because you have a strong personal stake in the matter. You may not be sentenced to prison, but you have imprisoned yourself!

It is interesting that legal systems in most parts of the world also take intention into account when determining the punishment for a crime. A cold-blooded premeditated murder is treated quite differently, for instance, from a crime of passion committed in the heat of the moment.

And yet *the karmic consequence is not a punishment*. The consequence is simply life's way of trying to work out the karma you are constantly creating. If you perform only negative mental karma, there may be no external consequence, but you experience a deeper level of internal suffering.

What does "working out karma" mean? It means that the play of your life is happening according to your tendencies, not according to some system of right and wrong. Your life simply organizes itself in order to fulfill your inclinations. Karma is not a punishment or reward; it is just the process by which life tries to fulfill itself.

A level of volition that many people are unaware of is action on the energy level. A negative thought, as we know, can breed karma. A negative thought combined with a negative emotion means a deeper karma. When a negative thought, negative emotion, and negative external action combine, there is even deeper karma. When a negative thought and negative emotion combine with a recurrent mental action, that karma is deeper still. (Killing someone in your head in a thousand different ways, as we saw, accumulates a great deal of karma.)

However, there are those who opt for energy-based action; this could mean engaging in practices that result in the death of an adversary or rival or any person they want to get out of the way. Such practices are known as occult or black magic. These occult systems exist on the fringes of many cultures, wherein a few experts can be approached to use their energies to cause harm to someone else. Once you energetically try to influence someone else for your own benefit, it is the worst possible karma. The karma generated by energy-based actions goes deeper than any other kind of action.

Let us not forget that what is right volition in one context might be markedly different in another. You have certain ideas of right and wrong because of the moral code of the society you live in. It is not your innate nature that dictates these codes. Society has certain fixed mores and rules, and whenever you flout them, you feel you have erred. You may never gamble before your parents, but you may do it quite easily with your friends. If you are found out by your parents, you immediately start feeling guilty.

Wearing a miniskirt in some parts of India may be considered outrageous. Similarly, being covered from top to toe in some parts of the world may be considered bizarre and inappropriate. These are not intrinsically right or wrong behaviors. It is society that deems what they are. However, if dressing differently from the social norm induces guilt or shame in the wearer, it could mean the accumulation of karma.

It happened.

Shankaran Pillai was on his deathbed. Knowing his end was near, he summoned his lawyer. He said, "I want to make a new will. I would like to leave my entire inheritance, down to the last dollar, to my wife. But I want to insist on just one precondition: she must marry within ninety days of my death."

The lawyer was surprised. "Why such a strange request, Mr. Pillai?" he asked.

"Well, I want at least one person to regret that I died!"

So what is very bitter for one person could be a blessing for another! One person's ideas of hell could be another's idea of heaven.

Ideas of right and wrong are inherently relative. For example, the Pindaris, a bandit tribe of India, were trained to rob and kill. The members of this tribe even had gods who taught them skills and brought them success in their banditry. When the British army was let loose on them, they were shot and killed indiscriminately. They were completely bewildered, because in their perception, they had done nothing wrong. The Pindari idea of virtue was simply to be a good bandit!

Thus it is not simply doing a deed that accumulates karma. It is *how* you do it, and with what motive it is performed, that makes all the difference.

Seeds of Volition

So what determines human volition? Why do some people operate out of a greater sense of inclusiveness and others out of a greater sense of exclusiveness?

Look at this closely. You will see that volition is shaped fundamentally by your belief that you are a separate being—an individual. In other words, it is your identification with your individuality that determines your volition.

The operative word here is *identification*. If you were not identified with this sense of separateness, you would not be accumulating karma. If your identification were all-inclusive, that would be the end of the karmic cycle!

Unfortunately, people's identification with narrow notions of individuality makes them engage with the world selectively rather than inclusively. The endless oscillation between like and dislike, attraction and aversion, further hardens their sense of separateness. Over time, likes and dislikes freeze into a personality and produce more karma. Individuality now becomes a prison rather than a privilege.

Gautama the Buddha's teachings on this subject—his emphasis on desirelessness, in particular—have unfortunately been misinterpreted and mutilated by many. Now, this was an incredibly perceptive man who would have known only too well that without desire, there can be no existence.

What he was pointing to was the importance of operating out of a state of inner fulfillment rather than inner hankering. Once this is accomplished, your life becomes *an expression of bliss, not a pursuit of it.* Your desire does not evaporate; instead, it becomes conscious. Your desire is no longer the unconscious fuel for your personal identity. It is the conscious tool by which you function. You will now desire the well-being of the entire planet.

The crux of the matter, therefore, is *identification* with your desires. When you are no longer identified with your desire, when there is a distance between you and your mind, you simply do what is needed for the moment and for the situation. You learn to play with desire. The desires are no longer about "you" anymore. Now your karmic bondage vanishes entirely.

How can one "dis-identify" with desire? How can there be desire without individuality, intention without identity? The logic is simple: individuality is a myth. It is an idea, not an existential reality. We have fragmented our world out of ignorance.

Once you are in touch with the foundation of intelligence that underlies all of creation, you realize that you are not separate from anyone or anything else. You are inseparably linked to the rest of this universe. Your body already knows that it is part of a great molecular dance of the cosmos. It knows that it will not survive for a moment without transacting with air, water, sunlight, and earth. Your mind, however, believes otherwise; it is convinced it is a limited entity. Therefore, any volition based on this limited understanding goes against the fundamental design of the source of creation. Any action that is impelled by such shortsighted and narrow volition invariably means karma. Or in other words, more compulsive existence.

Human beings have come to life on this planet with a tremendous possibility: that of absolute freedom. The yogic culture has reiterated this time and again. Every other animal has a fixed nature. They are simply operating on the basis of their instincts. This is why animals accumulate minimal karma. The human being, on the other hand, has come with the incredible capacity of transforming and transcending these instincts.

Unfortunately, most people do not have the necessary stability to remove themselves from the activity they are performing.

They are unable to act without a personal agenda. This is the crippling limitation they have imposed on themselves.

It happened.

On a certain day Shankaran Pillai went to the bar. He parked his donkey (which happened to be his mode of transport) outside. After downing a few drinks, he came out and found that someone had painted his donkey red. Shankaran Pillai was a very frail man, but now, with a couple of drinks inside him, he felt big.

He flew into a rage, strode back to the bar, kicked the doors open, and stood glaring around at everyone seated there.

"Who painted my donkey red?" he snarled.

A huge man, well over six feet tall, loomed up in a corner. "I did," he said.

Shankaran Pillai's manner changed instantly. He cleared his throat and said politely, "Sir, it is now ready for the second coat."

The above is, of course, an expedient reaction to a situation! Like most people, Shankaran Pillai's reaction was based on simple survival instinct in the face of a threat. There is a difference, however, between a reaction based on self-preservation and a response based on the intrinsic needs of a situation.

When your actions are no longer about you, when they are simply based on the demands of the situation, when narrow self-interest no longer fuels your volition, you have reached the end of karmic production. Your liberation is assured.

Of course, this is easier said than done. The problem is that people have forgotten *how to be inclusively involved* with life. Since their involvement is selective, they fall into the trap of entanglement. They either engage with life selectively, on the basis of their likes and dislikes, or opt for life-sapping philosophies of denial and detachment. In both cases, karma only multiplies.

Misconceptions of this kind are many. Many believe the Buddha preached that life is suffering, or *dukkha,* and conclude that his is therefore a dismal outlook of defeatism. What they overlook is that the Buddha spent his life trying to teach people meditation because he saw that humanity can *transcend* suffering. If he believed that suffering was all, he would have advised us to commit suicide! He saw that bliss—*ananda*—was a very real possibility. His life mission was to remind us of it.

A journalist recently asked me, "Do you agree that life is suffering?" I asked him, "If you had a choice, what would you want your life to be: suffering or bliss?" He immediately replied, "Bliss, of course." Ultimately, life is neither suffering nor bliss. It is *what you want it to be.* Life has no inherent quality whatsoever. The choice is always yours. The volition is always yours.

Adiyogi, the first yogi, was the first figure on this planet to assert that spiritual evolution is the great possibility, available only to humanity. The human being has come with the possibility of being a completely conscious being, rather than a compulsive one. We can choose to be whichever way we want: a tiger or a deer, a divinity or a demon. We have no fixed nature. Unfortunately, we suffer this fluidity, this phenomenal gift of freedom.

Most people have turned into human animals or creatures: not human beings. We have frittered away our freedom, bartered and sold it to external authorities, whether parental, religious, cultural, or political. Instead of exercising the freedom of consciousness, of choice, we have bought into the voices that have told us that to be human is to be limited, even sinful.

And so, instead of being the finest creatures on this planet, we have turned into the worst. We kill for pleasure, for love, for hatred, for identity, for God, for just about anything. Which other animal has unleashed so much wanton cruelty, animosity, and bloodshed on this planet?

Ironically, human volition—the source of our freedom—has turned into a curse. Instead of journeying from instinct to intelligence, from compulsion to consciousness, we have opted to regress. We have reached that point in our collective history where we have forgotten the enormous significance of being human. On an unconscious mission of self-destruction, we have compromised this extraordinary birthright of being the true masters of our life.

Avoidance Accelerates Karmic Accumulation

There is yet another unfortunate misunderstanding around karma and volition.

Since the endless oscillation between like and dislike creates karma, philosophies of avoidance and detachment have begun to grow popular. We have seen how Gautama the Buddha's teaching of desirelessness has been misinterpreted. All these philosophies and misinterpretations spring from a single impulse: to avoid karma.

The irony is that the more you try to avoid karma, the more it multiplies!

All the life-denying philosophies of detachment have developed because of the human fear of entanglement. What these philosophies overlook is that without an all-consuming, passionate involvement, there would be no life. What these philosophies end up denying altogether is life itself.

Philosophies of detachment are essentially joyless creeds. Embracing them might produce some semblance of balance and stability in day-to-day life, but they do not lead to liberation.

Instead, they frequently lead to greater karmic accumulation. Those who practice these life-denying philosophies turn slowly lifeless themselves. Inviting lifelessness is negative karma. The suppression of life is most definitely negative karma.

Now, what do we mean by suppression? Doing something you do not want to do is not necessarily suppression. Some traditions, for instance, encourage practitioners to fast at certain times. This is not suppression. People often think that not doing what they want to do at any given moment is suppression. This is not so.

Suppression simply means you are *experiencing life half-heartedly*. To live fully is to allow yourself to experience something totally. If you allow yourself to experience hunger totally, it is wonderful and liberating. If you allow yourself to experience food totally, it is also wonderful and liberating. Unfortunately, people do not experience either hunger or food totally. If you avoid any experience—whether pain or pleasure, sorrow or joy—it is big karma. But if you go through the experience without resisting it, the karma dissolves. This is why Krishna in the great Indian epic the *Mahabharata* says that hesitation is the worst of all crimes.

Today, in the name of civilization and etiquette, educated people often do not experience any of their emotions fully. They cannot cry fully. They cannot laugh loudly. Over a period of time, frustration sets in and they turn joyless. Their karmic accumulation also increases. You will see that simpler people who allow themselves to laugh and cry uninhibitedly as the impetus arises are often much freer. They work out their karma by experiencing each emotional state fully.

Living totally does not mean just having a good time. It means experiencing anything that comes your way fully and intensely. *The very process of life is the dissolution of karma.* If you live every moment of your life totally, you dissolve an enormous volume of karma.

Why Do Some People Suffer More Than Others?

Why didn't the universe create everyone equal? Why are some disabled, and others able-bodied? Why are some poor, and others rich? If there is a God, why didn't he create everyone equal? Why couldn't everyone carry positive karma? Why couldn't everyone have the same software? What is the point of all this terrible inequality?

These are questions that have plagued human beings since the dawn of time.

Now pause and examine this with absolute clarity.

If you do, you will see that the primary cause of human suffering is not physical handicap or poverty. The cause of human suffering is *oneself.*

Let us first make the distinction between pain and suffering. Pain is physical. Pain is produced whenever there is any injury to the body. Pain is the body's way of alerting you that something is wrong, that action must be taken. Pain is useful. It is a valuable wake-up call. Suffering, on the other hand, is psychological. It is produced by you. It is a hundred percent self-manufactured. You don't have a choice about being in pain, but you do have a choice about suffering. You can always choose *not* to suffer.

Let us look at this closely. A thousand years ago, people all over the world lived quite happily in modest dwellings. That was not a problem. The problem today is that someone lives in a mansion, and someone else lives in a one-bedroom apartment. That is the source of the latter's suffering. Someone has three cars, and someone else has one. That is the source of the latter's suffering. Someone vacations abroad, and someone else doesn't. That is the source of the latter's suffering.

So it is not the physical situation that causes misery. It is *the way you react to it*. Your karma is not in what is happening to you; your karma is in the way you respond to what is happening to you. Human beings are capable of suffering just about anything. Someone could not get into college, so they suffer. Someone else gets into college and can't get out, so they suffer! Someone cannot get a job, so they suffer. Someone is given a job, and now they suffer even more. Someone isn't married, so they suffer. Someone gets married, and they are in agony! Someone has no children, so they suffer. Someone has children, and so they are in constant torment. Your suffering is not because of your circumstances. Your suffering is because of the way you have made yourself. And *that* is what you need to look at.

But what about fate and fortune? What about the endless debate between free will and destiny? These questions still vex many people.

Whenever I am asked these questions, my first response is to point out that this argument can rage on forever. Do you want to spend your life debating it? Like the chicken-and-egg argument, it can go on until the end of time.

It happened.

One day, after a break of almost twenty-five years, Shankaran Pillai met up with a bunch of his college friends. They all gathered in a restaurant to celebrate. They ordered, and food and drinks came. As they were talking, naturally, the inevitable question came up: Which do you think comes first—the chicken or the egg? A huge debate began.

But as everyone was busy arguing, Shankaran Pillai was busy guzzling down his drink and eating whatever snack came his way. Then his friends asked, "Hey, are you not interested in such an important debate? Don't you want to know? Which do you think came first—the chicken or the egg?"

Shankaran Pillai looked up and said, "Whichever you ordered first will come first."

Do you really want to spend the rest of your life discussing free will and destiny?

In the East, we simply say "Your life is your karma." This means that how much karma you can take into your hands depends on how much of you has become conscious. If you have mastery over your physical body, fifteen to twenty percent of your life and destiny will be in your hands. If you have mastery over your psychological process, fifty to sixty percent of your life and destiny will be in your hands. If you have mastery over your very life energies, a hundred percent of your life and destiny could be in your hands.

Suppose I plant a mango seed. Can I expect that coconuts will fall out of the mango tree when it grows up? Can I expect cherries or apples? Now, that obviously would be absurd. If you plant a mango seed, you can expect only mangoes. That much is determined by the seed. But there are other considerations over which you do have control: How many mangoes will the tree yield? What will be the quality of the mangoes? How long will it yield them? Over these factors, you certainly do have control.

I should add a caveat. If you dig deep enough into life, you can change even the nature of the seed. But that takes a level of yogic accomplishment that is beyond the scope of this book. So that is a story we won't get into here.

What most people call luck is just your ability to be at the right place at the right time. Many of your capabilities are still unconscious, so you do not have complete control over the kind of circumstances you attract. But there is something over which you do have control: how you react to what happens to you.

Maybe you win a lottery ticket today, but, still, how happily you live is something you decide. A poor man might be ecstatic if he wins a million dollars. But a rich man might have much more in his bank balance and still be unhappy. So luck alone does not determine your happiness.

Generally, the word *karma* is used in a rudimentary way to suggest that you did something bad and so bad things will happen to you. This is a very limited and simplistic way of looking at life. Karma has nothing to do with moralistic categories of good and bad; it is related only to cause and effect.

If a man comes to you now and complains that his heart is clogged up, is it because he committed some terrible deeds in his past? No. It is much more likely that he lived irresponsibly, ate and drank improperly, and messed up his system. So this is bad karma in its own way, because he lived without the necessary understanding about how to treat his system. Ignorance is also a karma. As action is karma, inaction is also karma!

Someone recently came to me and told me about a dear friend of his who had lost the use of his hand. Now, the accident was unfortunate. But the real question is not about how many hands you have; the real question is whether you are suffering them.

Many Hindu gods and goddesses are presented in iconography and calendar art with four or more hands. It is highly likely that if you were granted four hands, you would suffer that as well. You wouldn't think you were a god; you would think you were a freak! And you would suffer that for sure.

I knew someone who had an extra finger and always had his hand stuffed in his pocket. Why? The finger didn't hurt; it had no problem. It was perfectly fine. The problem was just that everyone else has ten, so he felt weird. So it is not nine fingers or eleven that someone is suffering; it is just that he is creating his own suffering out of comparison. This is a psychological game.

Some seven miles from the Isha Yoga Center in Coimbatore, India, is a police station. About twenty-five years ago, it was manned by about eight to nine policemen; today it has about fourteen policemen. This station is in charge of a quarter of a million people. The police don't have a patrol car, and they don't carry guns. At any given time, around three to four policemen are on leave. Another three are on night duty. So only about seven to eight are actually at the police station. If you call them at night, one of them will ride over on a bicycle or else ask you to come to the police station to give a statement. You don't have much law enforcement machinery here, but you don't have much crime either.

Many of the villagers in this area lead economically impoverished lives but they are largely peaceful and happy people. They probably see people driving to the Isha Yoga Center in nice cars, sometimes in Mercedes-Benzes and Bentleys, but they aren't in despair or envy about their lot. There is the odd crime—usually a family feud or some caste clashes—but the incidence of felony or murder for money is extremely low. These people may not have a conscious spiritual process, but a certain ethos has percolated deep into their psyches. For them, this is their karma; they see their life as their doing, and so they feel no need to take something that belongs to another or to covet another's possessions.

Now, I do not want to romanticize poverty. One could argue that this kind of thinking could lead to fatalism and passivity. A certain dynamism certainly needs to be reinfused into the understanding of karma. It is important for people to feel that if their poverty is of their making, they can also turn it around.

Karma means that you can change your destiny, not simply be ruled by it. But at the same time, there is something wonderful about this ability to create joy in all kinds of circumstances. These people may be poor, but they are not suffering.

Suffering and misery are always by choice. Physical pain has, of course, to be handled in a very particular way. But suffering is only of the mind. If you are suffering mentally, it means that you are the source of your own suffering. You are the manufacturer of your own anguish.

The karmic substance within you may happen to contain all the necessary ingredients to create suffering. Perhaps you planted all these ingredients unconsciously in your past. So what can you do about this today? The answer is simple: *don't manufacture suffering for yourself today!* Maybe terrible things happened to you yesterday. Maybe you lost everything that is precious to you. But this morning when you get up, you still have the choice not to manufacture suffering for yourself. Yes, the ingredients of misery are present. They are waiting, perhaps even tempting you. But they cannot become suffering by themselves.

Suffering has to be freshly baked every day. In other words, your karma cannot turn into suffering without your cooperation. Once you are aware, that is the end of your suffering.

So the source of your misery is *not* your past actions. The source of your misery is how you're processing the imprint of the past now. You may be carrying around a sackful of stinking garbage. Either you can smear yourself with it and get terribly miserable, or you can make good manure out of it and create a wonderful garden.

Karma is the seed. What you are going to make out of this seed is entirely up to you. If I am given a packet of assorted seeds and I throw them all into my garden, perhaps all of them will sprout. Some of the mango seeds will yield very sweet fruit. But there may be some bitter seeds, too. The parthenium grass may be an unwelcome weed. And yet I still have the choice to pull it out. I can remove what is superfluous and keep the rest.

That is how your food is grown every day. A large part of agriculture is just weeding. There are actually more weeds than plants growing even in your own garden. If you keep weeding, you will have a garden. If you sit back defeated, you will have a patch of weeds. (Well, of course, some have learned to enjoy the weeds, too!)

The same holds true for your life. You have your seed karma. But you also have your weeding karma. This is where volition comes in. This is where intention becomes paramount. If you decide not to perform your weeding karma, your life will be just an overgrown wilderness. If you choose to perform this simple function, your life could yield an incredibly rich harvest.

Kula Vedana: The Weight of Collective Karma

Now, is there something like collective karma? Is the suffering of a parent transmitted to the child? Why do some clans and communities seem to suffer more than others?

Right now we may perform actions as individuals. But what we do can affect many other people as well. Our acts of intelligence and stupidity have collective consequences. If we chose to live high up in the mountains, the karma of wild animals might affect us more! But since we have chosen to live among people in social situations, other people's intentions and actions affect us. This becomes our collective karma.

There is something called *kula vedana*. This refers to the suffering of a collective, the suffering of a family, a clan, or a community. It means the suffering within you comes not just from your individual past. It comes from your forefathers and will be transmitted to your unborn children.

This is why traditional societies often maintained very strict demarcations in terms of intermarriage. These demarcations later developed into orthodoxy and social discrimination, and they are not relevant in today's world. However, their origins were rooted in a certain understanding. The crux of this issue was not just about genetics. It was based on the understanding that a certain karmic memory imprinted on your energy system is transmitted to your children and thereby perpetuates suffering. It means you are creating the kind of karma that will definitely have a negative impact on future generations.

Although these demarcations have no place in the modern world, many people are creating untold misery for future generations without being aware of it. Often a great deal of self-deception is involved. These people may be regarded as pillars of society, paragons of virtue, but their ideas or their way of living can spread suffering for generations after them. In their ignorance, they are contaminating not only their own lives but also those of their unborn offspring.

So how you live is not just about you. Whether previous generations are liberated from their karma and whether future generations do not suffer also depends on how you exist. The kind of grace you are fortunate enough to receive in your lifetime can also affect the lives of those before and after you.

The Indian epics have stories of kings who were born not to kings, but to sages. In this practice, called *niyoga*, the queen would have a child with a sage instead of her husband. This was done with the full knowledge of the king. The idea was to break the chain of suffering within a family. The king did not want his children to inherit all his negative karma; he wanted a son to be a better one than he could ever produce. Today this may seem outrageous and outlandish to us. But it was based on the simple logic that a kingdom deserved the best ruler. The king did not want to cripple or poison his offspring with his own suffering, his own greed, his own desire. He wanted the best for his people. Obviously this practice is outdated and irrelevant to modern times, as we have found democratic ways of choosing our leaders. But at the time it was based on a certain perception of how life happens.

If you go to a movie as a viewer, you may enjoy the entertainment—you may laugh, cry, eat your popcorn, and come out. But filmmakers view the whole drama differently. They know how the film is made; they know the craft behind it. A mere moviegoer will never understand how the film was created. The same is true of life. There were ancient wisdom traditions that understood how life worked, and certain practices that might seem strange to us today emerged from that perception.

There is a very simple aspect to collective karma as well. At the start of the twentieth century, the human population was 1.6 billion. As of August 2020, the world population was estimated at 7.8 billion. Here is an example of irresponsible karma. If we have multiplied at this rate, it is definitely our own doing. We cannot blame this on God's will.

I often relate an anecdote about the time I went to an international conference on poverty. As statistics were being shared about the millions of children who die every year without nourishment, one participant stood up and said, "But isn't all this divine will?"

I said, "Yes, if somebody else is starving to death, of course, it *must* be divine will. If someone else's children are dying of malnutrition, it *must* be a divine plan. But if *you* are starving, you will have your own plan, won't you?"

Unfortunately, we have twisted basic aspects of life around to suit our own distorted, self-serving logic. In the name of divin-ity, we have taken away even the humanity from human beings. There has been too much talk about divinity in this world. You don't have to talk about the divine. If you allow your humanity to overflow, the divine will happen. It has to happen. The aim should be to make yourself in such a way that you enslave the divine, not the other way around!

Karma means action. Whose action? *My* action. Whose responsibility? *My* responsibility. If you understand this simple formulation, karma will fall into place. No complex theory is necessary. Just look at it this way: "The way I am right now is of my making. The way I will be tomorrow will also be of my making." This is karma. This is the most dynamic way to exist.

Today, if a child walks before us without even basic nourish-ment in their body, this is our collective karma. It is our doing. As a society, as a generation, we have not done what we needed to do to nourish that child. Maybe we did not produce that child; the child is the consequence of the karma of two other individuals. But this is still our karma. Every time we see a malnourished child, a little pain happens within us. We cannot escape it. This *is* our karma.

We have the technologies at our disposal today that could either create phenomenal well-being or destroy the planet several times over. If the ignorant are empowered, they run the risk of sabotaging humanity entirely. It does not take a nuclear holocaust. We are capable of gassing ourselves without any nuclear assistance.

However, when each of us realizes the enormous conse-quences of our volition, thoughts, and actions, it could be the dawn of a great possibility: a conscious planet. We could now turn not merely into the architects of our own destiny but into collaborators in the collective destiny of the human race.

The Destiny Debate and the Astrology Argument

So what about fate, destiny, kismet? Do these play a role in determining our lives? Are the words relevant at all to our understanding of karma?

It is time to demolish some myths right away. What you call fate is just a life situation you have created for yourself unconsciously. Your destiny is what you have crafted in unawareness. If you become a hundred percent conscious, your destiny becomes a conscious creation. If you remain unconscious, you fall back on words like *fate* and *providence* to describe your predicament. It is as simple as that.

For every action that we perform there is a consequence. Whether the consequence bears fruit today or tomorrow or ten years later is irrelevant. The point is that it always bears fruit one way or another. So, some deeds you performed unconsciously many years ago may have their consequences today. You may choose to call it fate. But you could just as well call it your karma, your responsibility.

If you are diagnosed with hypertension right now, you might think "Oh, why did this happen to me? Why me? Why not my neighbor?" What most people don't acknowledge is that they have spent years of their lives routinely losing their temper. In modern society, it is considered perfectly natural to get angry five times a day! People can always find reasons that seem perfectly justifiable. But after years of doing this every day, is it any wonder that so many get high blood pressure? After years of polluting our planet and refusing to change lifestyles, is it any wonder that so many other diseases are rampant in our world today? Are we not collectively responsible for these? The fact is that people make their own lives and societies write their own self-destructive narratives, but we then try to pass the buck to

God or destiny. That may be convenient, but it is a foolish and immature way to exist.

Since fate is your unconscious creation, it is extremely important that every aspect of your life happen consciously. Otherwise you could go about poisoning your life without a clue about the damage you are inflicting on yourself.

This brings us to a related question: If we determine the course of our own lives, what about astrology? What about all those people who have had amazingly accurate predictions made about their future? What is the significance of the natal charts, or "horror-scopes," as I call them, that so many live their lives by? If the business of fortune-telling has endured for so many centuries, surely there must be some truth to it?

Now, astrology is simply a way of plotting certain possibilities in a person's life. If I look at you, because your karmic trajectory is immediately apparent to me, I am able to say "Okay, given your natural tendencies, this is the direction your life will take." There is nothing profound about this. Astrology is simply a possible road map for your life that takes into account your tendencies and inherited traits.

But consider this scenario. A thousand years ago, if you were a seafarer and the winds were blowing east, you would go east. Maybe you wanted to go to America, but you would end up in Japan. That was inevitable. The winds decided your destiny. Not anymore. Let the winds blow whichever way they want, today we still make sure we go where we want to go! We propel our own lives. We don't allow the winds to push us this way and that. Similarly, with the life process, if you are self-propelled, we say you are on a spiritual path. If you are being pushed around by your accumulated tendencies, your habits and your prejudices, then you are at the mercy of your horror-scope!

Traditionally, families in India turned to horoscopes because these would indicate a person's tendencies, karmic substance, the possible directions their life might take. Based on this astrological reading, a person would turn to a spiritual practice that enabled them to transcend these tendencies. But somewhere along the way, we dropped the technologies of transcendence and got stuck with just the horror-scope! This is an unfortunate state of affairs.

The spiritual practice is, by definition, always about taking your destiny in your own hands. If you want to fly, you might look at the weather—which way the winds are blowing, whether the rain clouds are coming your way, where the low-pressure areas are, and so on. Traditionally, people turned to astrology for the same reason. But the aim was always to write one's own destiny, not allow it to be written by one's inherited predispositions and vasanas.

The legendary story of Markandeya in Indian mythology is a testament to the determination to take charge of one's own life. Although his early death was predicted, this courageous young man triumphed over his own death. While he did seek grace to overcome his death, learning how to become available to grace is also karma. This is what it means to be spiritual. It means that you are now willing to take the very process of life and death into your hands. It means that you now say to yourself: "It doesn't matter who my forefathers were, what my karmic substance is. It doesn't matter what my past has been. I have decided the way I am going. I have determined that I am moving toward my liberation."

The horoscope was in any case meant only to be a way to navigate around possible obstacles. It was never meant to be a life script to be blindly followed. In fact, if you are on a spiritual path, authentic astrologers will never make predictions for you. Being spiritual means you are committed to charting your own destiny. When you are on such a path, what you are essentially saying to the world is "I am not windblown. I am self-propelled."

SADHANA

If you want to be self-propelled, it is important to start by fixing your intention. Make your intention as all-encompassing as you can. Start with a simple resolve. Decide to be a Mother to the World. That means seeing everyone as your own. There is no one who is not part of your clan. When you walk down the street, are you capable of looking upon everyone with the same sweetness of emotion that arises within you when you see your child coming home from school? This intention alone could liberate you from much agitation and negativity and could have a tremendous impact on how you craft your destiny.

If you are conscious every moment that everything and everyone on this planet is yours, you do not need any laws to tell you what you shall or shall not do. You have changed your fundamental identity. Your karmic boundaries now fall away and you experience a sense of boundlessness. A new identity of inclusiveness and involvement is born.

THREE

Karma as Memory

SUTRA #3

There is only one crime against life:
to make believe that you are something other than life.

The Mammoth Memory Bank

It happened.

One day Shankaran Pillai got very angry with his wife and left home. After wandering the streets for an entire night, he went to a restaurant for breakfast. When the server came to his table, he said, "Please serve me weak coffee, over-salted sambar*, and rock-hard idlis†."

The server was puzzled. "But sir, I can serve you some really hot and strong coffee, delicious sambar, and super-soft idlis."

---

* Lentil stew

† Dumplings made of rice and lentil batter

"You fool, do you think I've come here to enjoy breakfast?" asked Shankaran Pillai. "I'm just homesick!"

So it doesn't matter what it is—once you've gotten used to something, whether it is pleasant or unpleasant, you cannot drop it!

If it is volition that determines karma, the inevitable question is, From where does your volition arise?

As we have seen, it is from your identification with the notion of separateness.

From where then does this identification arise?

From memory.

You believe you are an individual because your memory tells you that this is who you are.

Perhaps it would be more accurate and more useful, therefore, to describe karma as memory.

Think about it. Everything you consider to be yourself is a result of memory. What you call "me" is a product—in every sense of the term—of your past.

Everything that has ever come into contact with you through these five sense organs—whatever you saw, heard, smelled, tasted, and touched—is there in your memory, influencing your personality. Every bit of memory that you gathered in wakefulness and in sleep is in this bank.

Whether you are conscious of it or not, every cell in your body remembers and acts out of that memory every moment of your life. Life is telling you about your karma at every instant. The problem is that you listen only to your thoughts or to your neighbors! If you listened to the life process, no teaching, no scripture would ever be necessary.

Karma is one big noise. If you cannot hear it, it is simply because right now you are accustomed to listening to the outer world. But once you learn to listen to your interiority, you hear the karmic din loud and clear. The decibel levels are so high, there's no missing it!

Your body is a heap of food you have ingested over time. Your mind is a heap of impressions and ideas you have imbibed and processed over time. Both are creations of the past. Both are products of memory. So whether you identify with your body or your mind, what you call your personality is simply an accumulation of memory. The essence of *everything you consider to be yourself is karmic.*

Right now, if you walk from your home a couple of blocks down the street, a hundred different smells assail you. You may not be conscious of these. Only if a very strong smell comes your way will you notice it. But all the hundred varieties of smells that your nostrils have come in touch with unconsciously have actually been recorded in your memory.

Experiments have been conducted that substantiate this: Someone who knows no Chinese, for instance, is exposed to the language when they are in deep sleep. Years later, under certain conditions of hypnosis, they can actually utter the same ten sentences in Chinese that they heard while they were asleep. That is how memory works; the systems of body, mind, and energy are simply soaking in information every moment.

You may not remember consciously what happened twenty-five years ago, but it is working on you. What happened twenty-five hundred years ago is still imprinted on your body. What happened twenty-five million years ago is still encrypted in your body. Everything that ever happened on this planet is still remembered by your body, because your body is just a piece of this planet.

The memory from the very beginning of creation is right *here.* Your mind might have forgotten life as a unicellular being, but your body still remembers. Your mind might have forgotten your great-grandmother, but her nose still sits on your face. You could dismiss this as genetics. But genetics, as we have seen before, is essentially memory. People think memory means only mind. But that is not the case. The volume of memory that the body carries is a billion times more than the volume of memory your mind is capable of carrying.

The rocks and trees and various objects around you are throwing out different vibrations right now. Every pebble, every stone, is saying something. The problem is only that most people are not sensitive enough to hear them or do not possess enough attention to decipher their language.

Now, if all the levels of memory in you were wiped out this instant, you would have no personality at all. The differences in people's personalities are entirely due to memory—physical, mental, energetic. As this memory acts itself out, you become an automaton working according to the diktats of your past karma. Your ability to use your discerning mind diminishes gradually, and your ability to choose is impeded.

As karmic bondage builds up, you will naturally try to draw smaller and smaller circles around yourself. At the age of eighteen, most people draw large circles; by the age of seventy, the circles shrink, and people find that they can get along with only a few. By drawing karmic circles, you determine the boundaries of your responsibility. As you keep shrinking these boundaries, you are heading straight toward depression. And yet the human problem is that you are constantly labeling your bondage as freedom!

There is a simple way to check if you are increasing or decreasing the size of your karmic circle. When life situations place you in unfamiliar or unexpected terrain, what is your reaction? If you are asked to dress differently for an occasion, or if you find you have misplaced your keys, or if your footwear accidentally walks off with someone else, or if you check into a hotel and find you have to sleep on mattresses on the floor, how would you react? These are small triggers. Think of larger ones, and ask yourself what your reaction would be. If the very thought of these situations makes you anxious, you inhabit a very constricted karmic space.

These unconscious reactions become the unexamined aspects of your personality. Over time, these patterns grow more rigid and frozen, and so you say "Oh, this is the kind of person I am. This is my personality." Someone might offer you a better way to live, but you find yourself shrugging it off and saying "No, no, but this is the way I am."

Hasn't it happened to you any number of times? You made up your mind: "I'm going to make this change in my life." For three days, you were transformed; on the fourth day, you were back in the same old rut! Although you tried to choose differently, your old patterns ended up ruling.

When you were eighteen, it looked like you could grow in so many different ways. But as you grew older, it slowly seemed like choices were shrinking. It felt like there was only one way for you to be. As the karmic substance increases in volume, the discerning mind becomes almost useless, because you now work largely by habits, patterns, and cycles.

The attraction to one's own karmic patterns can be powerful, because most people experience a sense of safety in the familiar. Whether the patterns or cycles are small or big is irrelevant. Their recurrence can offer a sense of security, identity, and even power for those who fear the unfamiliar.

It happened.

In the year 2009, a lion in the forest ambled over to a pig and bragged, "Look at me! I'm the king of the jungle. If I roar, the entire jungle trembles in fear."

The pig laughed and said, "That's no big deal. If I sneeze, the entire world will tremble in fear right now."

The business of identity (as the pig during the swine flu pandemic was clearly very aware of) definitely wields more power than ever before!

So if you have to break the tyranny of karmic memory, you have to crack the karmic substance. Otherwise, since you have come here as a human being, with this level of intelligence and awareness, it is tragic to forego the great human power of choice.

Human Beings as Bags of Karma

When I was age four or five, I often saw people as hazy forms. If I just sat down in the living room and looked around at my family—my mother, father, brother, sisters—I would see them as hazy beings, like ghosts, moving here and there. If I was moving around or talking, they appeared as people. But if I simply sat, I would see them as smoky figures floating around. And once you see people as semi-solid smoky beings, the whole drama of everyday life becomes utterly meaningless. Suddenly, my dad would come and ask, "What about your mathematics quarterly exam?" I had no idea what he was talking about! It was like watching television after pressing the Mute button.

One of the things that did not really make much of an impression on me was a person's gender. This would not register in my mind for a long time. Even later in my life, I never paid very much attention to the physical form of a person. What always drew my attention was a larger, hazier form that I could clearly see around them. I never felt the need to define these forms to myself. But I realized later that these were energy bodies that every living being carries. In yogic terminology, this is termed the *pranamayakosha*. It is possible to clearly see karma imprinted on this level.

This may be difficult to grasp, but my mind is never inclined to understand anything that I see. If I don't see clearly, I look at something a little more attentively, but I don't make an effort to understand something intellectually. If you want to see keenly, you simply learn to sharpen your perception. If you look at a tree keenly enough, for instance, you don't need to read a gardening manual—you can assess whether it has received enough sunlight or water. (Of course, a sad irony today is that many sit under a tree and choose to read a book on trees instead of learning from the tree itself!)

That is what the yogic discipline is all about: just learning to look. This is why I keep telling people around me: Don't look for anything. Don't look for the meaning of life. Don't look for God. *Just look*—that's all. This is the fundamental quality of a spiritual seeker, as life is about seeing what is there, not about seeing what you want to see.

Since people are so identified with their own individuality, shaped by their karmic substance, they reflect the same limitations. They see everybody as limited individuals because they see themselves the same way. Instead of seeing life as just life, they identify with fragments of it.

The time has come for human beings to transcend the distorting lens of karma—the lens that makes them confuse the projection for the real, their fragmented, memory-driven psychological creation for the incredible majesty of life itself. The time has come to wake up to the fact that there is *only one crime against life*: to make believe that you are something other than life. Unfortunately, our idea of individuality is separateness, and that is the basis of all suffering.

Just as inherent power of enormous proportions resides in every atom (enough to unleash unimaginable destruction), the inherent power of human intelligence has similarly been broken down into atomized forms of thought and emotion. These have become a source of unspeakable suffering and destruction. Ask Mother Earth—for sure she will agree! Our identification with our separateness has broken down this magnificent creation and shattered the universality of our lives.

Eventually, however, *it is the universal that prevails,* not our fragmented identities. In the ultimate scheme of things, human beings count for nothing. Even if you destroy the planet, it means nothing. Creation is like a video game: Once it is over, nothing is left on the screen. Not even a flicker to suggest what once was.

And so, with no intention of demeaning human beings, let me say that when I looked at people, I saw them only as bags of karma. I still do. Some are huge sacks; some are small bags; some are just an envelope. The nature of the load may be different in terms of quality and impact. Lighter karmic content brings life to ease. And how you deal with each individual naturally arranges itself based on this. When you are karmically lightweight, people approach you with much greater ease.

If a hundred people are sitting before me right now and I focus on one person, I can feel their specific vibration separately, and with that I know their entire karma. I may not know what they did in a previous life, whether they married, had children. I may not know the details. But I know the quality of their karma. I know whether the dominant quality is hatred or anger or peace. The moment I see a person, I know that. To know the details, one needs to enter a person's unconscious mind: this is a different dimension. But simply seeing the karmic bag can give me a feel of their karma.

However, whether it is a large sack, a smaller bag, or an envelope does not necessarily mean less or more karma. It is the *density* of the material that makes a difference. In fact, an envelope may contain much more karma than any sack can contain, but the difference is of refinement. Karmic substance gathered in fear, anger, hatred, and jealousy will create a density that makes it hard to carry and also hard to approach. And hence the whole tradition of dividing karma into good and bad is a facile demarcation. But the more refined load is undeniably easier to carry. A sack could contain loose cotton; an envelope could have the weight of an epic!

There have been many people to whom I had said in no uncertain terms (sometimes even more than a decade in advance) that certain health issues or accidents or loss of fortune would befall them. I was not giving them an astrological prediction of doom. It was simply a perception based on looking at their karmic trajectory. These were not intrinsically good or bad events. They were occurrences in their trajectory that could be altered either by distancing oneself from the events or by performing alternative karmas to counteract them.

I myself carry a million times more karma than most people. This is because I consciously remember several lifetimes. But I do not carry this as a burden. If you look at most intellectuals in this world, you will see that they have become heavy with memory. I carry much more memory than most, but I am not encumbered by it, because I carry my karma at a distance from myself. I can access it when I need it, but I do not carry the load upon myself all the time. With practice, everyone is capable of this. It is similar to the cloud on which we now store our computer files—accessible when we need it, but that does not clutter our hard disk. Thus I do have access to lifetimes of memory, but it is all on a "cloud"!

Membranes of Memory

The yogic tradition has an elaborate method of differentiating memory. It distinguishes between eight dimensions, or "membranes," of memory: elemental, atomic, evolutionary, genetic, karmic, sensory, articulate, and inarticulate.

All eight can be seen essentially as human karma. The first four are types of memory in which personal volition plays no role. The next four are those in which personal volition does play a role. In other words, the first four constitute our collective karma; the next four constitute our *individual karma*.

Let us examine the first four aspects of memory, the ones in which personal volition plays no role:

Elemental memory refers to the way the building blocks of your system—earth, water, fire, air, and ether—shape who you are. They carry with them memories from the very beginning of creation.

Atomic memory—the fluctuating patterns of atoms that make up your body—molds your system further.

Evolutionary memory hones your biology: It is this evolutionary software that makes you a human being, for instance, and not an animal. Even if you eat dog food, you remain a human being! This evolutionary code is imprinted deeply upon your DNA.

What is your body anyway? As we have seen, it is just an accumulation of food, water, and air you have absorbed from the planet. The substance you call earth and the substance you call body are not different. But a complex amalgam of memories transforms the substance beyond recognition. The same soil becomes food when you ingest it, nourishes you, and makes you a human being rather than a plant or a dog. The privilege of being a human being in this life is mainly due to evolutionary memory.

The same external elements of water, air, and food behave differently within each human being. As soon as you ingest them, they begin to work in very different ways. The water in a bottle is very different from the water inside your system. The fruit outside you behaves very differently once it is within you. The transformation is mainly because of the interplay of atomic, elemental, and evolutionary memory within you.

Certain dimensions of memory are shared by all of us: the elemental, the atomic, and the evolutionary. However, our genetic and personal karmas are different. Genetic memory is passed on within families, determining several shared physical and psychological characteristics.

Beyond these four types of memory, which make up our *collective karma*, are the four types of memory in which our personal volition does play a role: they make up our *individual karma*.

First is our *personal karmic memory*: the blitzkrieg of impressions that have shaped us over time and turned us into distinctive human beings, each with our own quirks and idiosyncrasies, likes and dislikes, habits and preferences. Every human being carries a vast storehouse of personal karmic memory, which is why no two human beings, even twins, are ever completely alike.

Our daily negotiation with our immediate physical and cultural environment also has an impact upon our system, determining the way our bodies and minds respond to the world and creating *sensory memory*.

And then, we have *inarticulate memory*, the enormous reservoir of generic and specific information accumulated over eons, of which we are not aware. It is a base, akin to the foundation of a house, and silently influences how you gather *articulate memory*—your superstructure. Articulate memory is the impact of all the conscious information that every human being carries within.

These eight dimensions of memory are not separate membranes. They are deeply interlinked, and it is these interconnections that are responsible for the breathtaking diversity of the human beings we see around us. These membranes constitute the entire volume of a human being's karma.

Evolution is accumulated memory constantly building upon itself to reach higher and higher possibilities of life. But human beings, being the very peak of evolution, can transcend this entire volume of accumulated memory and become the architects of their own destinies.

When the Dead Live Through You

At a program I conducted recently in Los Angeles, I saw four female participants who looked similar. They were not sisters. They simply shared the same doctor! So, there are ingenious ways by which we can reshape our genetic inheritance today.

Traditionally in India, the term *samskara i*s used to describe the enduring impact of our genetic memory on our present. Your body actually carries a trillion times more memory than your mind. The word *samskara* denotes the maelstrom of hereditary memories and impressions that are bequeathed to us by our ancestors, our clan, or our tribe.

And so, when a child sings exceptionally well, for instance, it is common for people to say "Oh, that is their samskara." That means that this particular gift has come to the child from their gene pool, their ancestral learning.

These genetic memories are not inherently positive or negative. It is how we deal with them that makes the difference. We carry the memories of our ancestors within us. But whether this memory has become a source of bondage or one of advantage depends on how much distance we have created from it.

The dead are trying to live through you in a host of different ways. Make no mistake about it. Look at your own life, or at the lives of those around you. For many people, having children is a way of immortalizing their genetic material, a way of ensuring that they live on after their time. This is their legacy—one that they hope will live on for posterity. So do not underestimate your ancestors either! They are also trying to live through you. This is the self-perpetuating nature of genetic memory. We owe a great deal to our ancestors. But if we are to live on this planet as independent full-fledged lives—not as puppets of our forebears—we must first find ways of becoming individuals.

Now, though the spiritual process is about dissolving the myth of separateness, an important first step on the path is to become an individual. This may seem to be a paradox, but it is not so. When you are the consequence of many influences, you are a crowd. When you are a crowd or clan of influences, transformation is impossible. Crowds can evolve over a period of time, but they cannot be transformed. Transformation, as the word suggests, necessitates a form. Only an individual can be transformed, or transcend the narrow identification with separateness. It is impossible for a collective to ever be enlightened. Enlightenment can happen only to an individual.

I often joke that only two types of ghosts exist: those without a body and those with one! Most human beings are simply ghosts with bodies. In short, they are phantoms of their past. Their lives are simply programmed by their ancestral memory.

Samskara is important because it is a reminder that we are shaped by memory on many subtle levels that we are not even aware of. You may not be conscious of it, but something within a human being deeply resents the loss of freedom.

The most searing reminder of this is in prison life. I have witnessed this firsthand when I was conducting programs in prisons. The interesting thing about prisons is that they can actually be pretty well organized. The food comes on time; you are given clothing and shelter; the lights are turned on and off for you; doors are opened for you and, of course, closed after you! For some people who live pretty poorly outside, prison life is a structured alternative. And yet if you enter a prison, you feel the pain in the air. This is a deep, inexplicable pain, because security has been given but freedom has been taken away. The loss of freedom is the deepest suffering for a human being.

Whether your freedom is taken away by a prison, by your own samskaras, or by genetic or evolutionary memory doesn't really matter. Either way, you will find, after a while, that your life will be permeated by unexplained suffering. You will not know why, but your entire existence will seem stifling, repetitive, constraining.

A landmark experiment at Emory University in Atlanta in 2013 established an interesting finding. The fragrance of cherry blossoms was introduced into a cage of mice. At the same time, a mild electric shock was repeatedly administered to the mice. After some time, there was no need for the shock. Merely at the smell of cherry blossoms, the mice would run in the opposite direction in fear.

The amazing thing, however, was that the reaction of fear held true for the next generation of mice as well. When this new generation encountered the smell of cherry blossoms, they experienced the same fear and recoiled from it. This was without any personal experience of the electric shock. A heightened sensitivity to the fragrance continued in the second and third generation as well.

This milestone experiment is a reminder of how insidiously samskaras can work. It is a reminder of how your impressions today can influence generations after you. You need genetic memory for survival, continuity, and well-being, but you also need a distance from it to live a life of consciousness, joy, and freedom.

But how do you create distance from a memory that you are not even conscious of? How do you step away from memory that throbs, unknown to you, in every cell of your body?

Indian spiritual traditions created an elaborate science around making use of genetic memory in a way that can enhance human capability and success. On the other hand, this science also enables us to consciously distance ourselves from genetic memory in a manner that supports our spiritual growth and liberation.

On one level, there are special rituals and practices (referred to as *karmas* or, when performed at a deeper level, as *kriyas*) that are immediately performed for the dead by their families. These practices refer to ways by which we honor the memory of those we love and, at the same time, strive to become free of their influence. These rituals are performed not just for the generation before us. They can be done for twelve generations in some cases, or for seven, or at least for three.

Every culture has variations of these rituals. Jesus urged his disciples to leave the dead to the dead. And we have to do so if we seek to become truly alive. These rituals signify our desire to wipe our slates clean. They are our ways of saying that we do not want to live out recycled lives. We want to start fresh. We want to write our own scripts.

In addition to the death rituals, certain yogic practices can be hugely empowering. A spiritual initiation is an intervention on the level of the energy body that separates you from your genetic memory in a certain way.

This is also why many powerfully energized physical forms were consecrated in the Indian subcontinent as deities created for the well-being of a particular clan or community. When one person performed a ritual or process for that energy form, all the people from that genetic pool benefited from it. Today, when these close-knit groups are dissipating and the genetic pool is more mixed than ever before, many of these deities have grown largely irrelevant. But there was a very real technology involved in their making.

This is theoretically possible with certain yogic practices as well. If you take a hundred people from the same genetic pool and teach powerful yogic practices to ten of them, you could well find, in thirty months or more, all one hundred people manifesting the benefits of this yoga. That may sound strange, but it is very much possible in situations of genetic commonality and geographic proximity. When a person is touched on the level of the etheric body (*vignanamayakosha* in yogic terminology), it is possible for them to influence others who share the same samskaras. This is more difficult in the modern world, where communities are more mixed and scattered than ever before. But the benefits of an initiation on the etheric level can still impact others in the larger family context today, even if the impact is to a lesser extent.

In traditional Indian culture, there were also elaborate guidelines for a pregnant woman—the kind of foods she should eat, the kind of situations and atmospheres she should be exposed to. These detailed guidelines around conception and pregnancy were very much part of the Eastern cultures because they knew the mechanisms by which samskaras could be transmitted generationally.

One of the fundamental responsibilities for each generation is to realize that we are just baton carriers. We are simply handing over the baton from the earlier generation to the next. It is our responsibility to hand over a better planet. Ecologically, it is no longer possible to hand over a better planet, so we have, unfortunately, already failed at this duty. We may bring some improvement, but we cannot return things to the way they were.

But we also have another responsibility: to create a better generation of human beings. We can accomplish this only if we truly care about who we are today. Since memory is constantly transmitting itself in so many different ways, it is our duty to support the next generation by first taking responsibility for our own.

When you live by the memory of a single book, you are religious. When you live by the memory of several books, you are intellectual. When you live by the memory of several generations of people, you become a truly compassionate human being. But *when you live beyond the memory of generations of people, you become a mystic.*

Those who share our genes absorb our legacies so much more easily than others. However, the science of yoga is about raising yourself to a place where your genetic memory has no influence upon you whatsoever. Now you become what the world regards as a seer—someone who sees ahead with piercing clarity and insight. With deepening yogic practice, you find your samskaras are no longer limited by categories of class, tribe, or community. You are now capable of influencing just about anybody. As a world citizen, your bequest becomes truly global.

Runanubandha: The Honey Trap of Physical Memory

What is the role of committed relationships in a fast-changing world? How necessary are they? Has commitment outlived its utility? Has it outgrown its relevance?

These are questions I am often asked.

While these may seem to be sociological questions, a very

real karmic aspect is involved here. Committed relationships and marriage are social arrangements. Therefore, their value may seem to be only social. However, the capacity of the human body to remember is enormous. The implications of this memory for human life are tremendous, too.

This is not a moral argument. It is based on very simple sense. Your body is brimming with memory: *everything* about it is the result of programming, from its shape and color to its texture and size. This is why you still have your great-grandmother's arthritic knee and find it difficult to erase your monkey ancestor's habits! (Don't forget: a human being and a chimp share 98.6 percent of their DNA!)

Now, body memory works on all the levels we have discussed earlier in this chapter. But a very important and large aspect of this memory is *physical* (as distinct from psychological and energetic). In Sanskrit, this physical memory of the body is called *runanubandha*. Runanubandha is the physical memory you carry within you. It is a result of blood relationships, as we have seen earlier, but also, more important, a result of sexual relationships.

Wherever there is physical intimacy—particularly of a sexual nature—the body registers the memory deeply. And so the arrangement of committed relationships in any society is based on a bedrock of profound intelligence. The logic is simple: since a significant exchange of memory occurs in any physical encounter, if you confuse the body's memory with too many physical impressions, your system grows confused. Once your memory system becomes complicated, it could take a lot more work to settle your life.

It is important to emphasize that there is nothing wrong with runanubandha. It is an essential part of life. Without runanubandha between a couple, for instance, a future generation could not be perpetuated. And without runanubandha between a mother and child, a child could not survive. The only question, however, is how to make it supportive rather than entangling; how to ensure, in short, that a bond does not turn into bondage.

For anyone on a spiritual path, simplifying runanubandha becomes particularly important, because the ultimate aim for the seeker is to transcend physicality. If one nurses such an intention, it is wise to keep the body as a simple process, uncluttered by the encumbrance of too much memory. For only if physical memory is kept minimal can the spiritual begin to unfold.

The implications of physical memory are many. The sexual act creates maximum runanubandha between people. In this exchange, the female body, being more receptive, registers physical intimacy much more deeply than the male. When the woman bears a child, a large part of this memory is downloaded onto her offspring. This explains a common occurrence: when a woman becomes pregnant, her partner often becomes a much less important presence in her life. That is because a deep transference of memory—in terms of genetic and physical karma— is taking place for a new generation to be created. The earlier receptivity to her partner is replaced by her new role as a transmitter of physical memory to her offspring.

Women also often notice that when they get pregnant, the intensity of their feelings for their parents and other people who were very important to them begins to decline. The level of emotional attachment in other relationships often begins to dip. This is Nature's system at work: If the body remembers its own parentage too much, it will not be able to house the new child— who is of different genetic material—as effectively. If there is too much memory, there will be struggles within the body.

As we have seen, the Sanskrit term *kula vedana* (collective suffering) implies that the whole clan's memory runs through you. Your body tends to behave in a particular way because it is the carrier of these deep physical memories that make up the suffering of your people, your tribe. If you complicate your system with further runanubandha, the suffering can be enormous.

Now, let us distinguish between the memory of the mind and the memory of the body. When the mind encounters memory, a certain amount of discernment is involved. But the body takes on memory without discernment. Take the example of food: your mind can discern whether something is nourishing, but the body only can taste and then either get sick or be nourished. It is the same with physical relationships. The mind has some measure of discernment about a partner, but the body does not. It simply receives.

What the body does have, however, unlike the mind, is *the ability to perceive.* The mind can compute, calculate, process, assess, but it is not an instrument of perception. The mind simply interprets what the body perceives. Sharpening the body's ability to perceive is the whole purpose of yoga. When your hard disk is full, you cannot take in any more memory; it is already memory saturated. But when the body is uncluttered, it becomes a tremendous tool. If you simplify and reduce the volume of physical memory through yoga, the body can turn into a powerful instrument of perception.

For instance, if a plate of food is placed in front of me, if I simply put my hands over it, I know how the food will behave inside my system. Depending on what I need to do that day— whether it is initiating a group into a kriya or playing a game of golf—I will decide whether to eat the food or not. It is possible to cultivate the body in such a way that its perception is razor-sharp. To develop such discernment, however, the memory's impact on the physical body needs to be minimal.

When yogis choose a place as a site of practice, they will usually walk around the area for a while, get a feel of the space, and then choose a particular spot. That is how sensitive their body has become; it can discern what spot is suitable for spiritual practice.

Their choices have nothing to do with personal likes or dislikes. There is a certain New Age impulse to speak of positive energy and negative energy somewhat indiscriminately. Many people say "I don't like the vibe" of a person or a place without a clue of what that means. It usually means that they have likes and dislikes and have not yet transcended them. For the yogi, the discernment of the body has nothing to do with personal attraction or aversion, craving or recoil, likes or dislikes. The body for the yogi is as clinical and impersonal as a barometer—it does not judge; it simply perceives.

So, to return to the question of relationships, does this imply that a committed relationship is natural? *Natural* is not the appropriate word. But we could deepen our understanding of what natural means. You could think of it this way. Nature works on many different levels. One aspect of nature is purely physical. If you go according to the diktats of physical nature, you might want to mate with just about anyone. But other dimensions of nature exist within you as well. If you move into another dimension, where emotional intimacy becomes important, and if you fall head over heels in love with another person, a monogamous relationship is fine.

If you step into an even more profound dimension, you do not want contact with even one other person; you simply want to be left alone. This is because you have experienced the body as a complete life process. You realize that it does not need another body to support it. You do not want to disturb this process by involving another body. You want to keep it as it is. So there are many levels of nature within you. It all depends on what level you are living at.

It is in an attempt to reach the deeper dimensions of nature that ascetic traditions developed all over the world. Sexuality is a very big way of building memory. The reason people go into asceticism is not because they are against sex, or are anti-pleasure. It is because they do not want to add any new memory into their system. This body already remembers too much. They know that the old karma—which is quite a big heap—needs to be worked at. And that is the work of a lifetime.

Without dropping physical memory, the body is ridden with compulsions. Most people are aware of this. You may decide with great determination to abstain from certain substances or to wake up early every morning. You may even manage for a while, but that is only in the initial phase. Mental determination alone cannot eradicate physical memory. It takes time and effort to work runanubandha out of your system.

You can see how difficult it is already. So many triggers exist. The memory of tobacco may provoke the body to move in one direction; the smell of alcohol in another; the aroma of food in one direction; the memory of sexuality in yet another.

Once all these memories have been reduced, however, life is very simple. Now if you want to simply sit still, the body does this very easily. Life now unfolds in the best possible way. With unexamined accumulation, the body can turn into a living hell. But once this receptacle is reasonably empty, once there is a certain ease in the system, this body is extraordinarily perceptive.

SADHANA

If you want to test your own levels of runanubandha, you could try sitting alone in an unfamiliar place on an unfamiliar piece of furniture. Observe yourself closely. How comfortable is your body? Is it uneasy? Does it seem to want to be elsewhere? You may have noticed that older people often have a favorite armchair. In many families, people gravitate toward the same chairs at the dining table. Some of this is a matter of convenience or habit. But very often what is at work is runanubandha.

The more runanubandha you build, you can be sure you are moving backward on the ladder of spiritual evolution. Karma sets a boundary for you. When that boundary becomes too comfortable, it is time to start becoming vigilant. The same chair or room may give you physical privacy, but if you find yourself growing territorial about it or disturbed as if your very identity depends on it, it is time to start shaking up your karma.

The reason many spiritual traditions offered monasteries and ashrams to seekers was to enable them to live in a circumscribed geographical place that was free of runanubandha. This sometimes created a new set of boundaries and territories, which is unfortunate. But the aim was always to empower the seeker to expand horizons, rather than to contract them. In the outside world, their runanubandha would often draw them to a certain set of people or places or circumstances over and over again. *Kshetra sanyas*—a Sanskrit term that refers to a vow to never leave a certain consecrated geographical space—was a way for seekers to liberate themselves from the overpowering tentacles of physical memory.

FOUR

The Great Karmic Warehouse

SUTRA #4

*However profound it is, everything that
comes from memory spells karmic bondage.*

Categories of Consequence

In the previous chapter, we looked at the eight membranes of memory: four of which are collective and four of which are individual.

However, the yogic system now leads us deeper into an exploration of individual karma. If you find yourself overwhelmed by the classifications that follow, do not get disheartened. As a reader, you do *not* have to remember these categories in order to decode karma. It would certainly be easy to dispense with these classifications to make a karma book a simpler, breezier read. But if I include them, it is to reveal the incredible intellectual precision and sophistication of which the ancient yogis and sages were capable. Even if you were to simply read these categories without making any attempt to remember them, you would have a deeper and richer understanding of the subject. The workings of karma are complex, but the classification is a simple one.

Let us take a look at four essential categories of karma, or consequence.

Behind every individual is one vast storehouse of karma—the sum total of accumulated memory, in Sanskrit termed *sanchita*. For our purpose, let us simply call it Accumulated Karma. This is like a great warehouse in which all eight types of memory are contained: elemental, atomic, evolutionary, genetic, individual karmic, sensory, articulate, and inarticulate.

We carry this enormous volume of information with us all the time. The quantity might vary, but every human being carries this phenomenal karmic inheritance.

Now, within this vast storehouse of accumulated memory, there is an important dimension called Allotted Karma. This, in turn, contains two aspects. Let us call them Actionable Karma in the Present, and Actionable Karma in the Future.

Let us look at what these terms imply.

From the vast storehouse of *sanchita*, a segment of memory ripens. It surfaces and comes to the fore, demanding immediate attention. This is your Allotted Karma. Every human being has a certain allotment of karma for a lifetime, called *prarabdha karma* in the Indian tradition: it is the karma that needs to be handled *now*. The rest continues to remain latent and unripe, in the vast storehouse of accumulated memory.

So your current lifetime is a certain allotment of karma—a distinct amount of memory—playing itself out. The nature of this allotment varies from person to person. For each person, the life energy works differently. Each person has a different percentage of energy dedicated to physical activity; a different percentage to intellectual activity; a different percentage to emotional activity; a different percentage to energy activity; and a different percentage to the capacity for meditativeness, or inner stillness.

The nature of a person's allotment is actually visible at an early age. Parents can see it clearly in two children. One may have a certain propensity for physical activity, while the other may be quieter. These differences are sometimes even subtly visible in newborn infants in a hospital maternity ward! Later, of course, differences grow because of the type of environment the child grows up in—the food they eat, the type of attitudes they develop. But very early differences are determined by the nature of each child's Allotted Karma.

Now, every spiritual process is essentially about digging into the storehouse of Accumulated Karma. Spiritual practitioners are people in a hurry. They want to dig up as much as possible and work it out, rather than wait for each allotment to ripen in its own time. This is why so much of the spiritual process is action oriented. Spiritual seekers want to handle ten lifetimes of karma in a single lifetime if they can. The spiritual journey also teaches them to avoid accumulating new karma and to limit the consequences of their Allotted Karma. In this manner, they work through large karmic volumes at great speed.

How does one feel when one has emptied out one's Allotted Karma? Usually, life grows more relaxed, less reactive, less compulsive. Strong likes and dislikes, whether about people, places, food, work, or politics, begin to weaken; comfort zones become less important. Initially, you may find you want to slow down and live quietly. After that, you will choose to engage with the world again, but this time it will be in a wonderfully conscious way. Your life is now full of choices.

We now come to another aspect of Allotted Karma. This is Actionable Karma in the Present (*kriyamana karma*), or karma that compels outward action. We cannot resist its power. There are many impulses and propensities in a human being, but not all of them propel us to external action. However, every individual carries another type of karma that *must* be acted upon externally. The rest can be handled internally. How you handle your externally Actionable Karma in the Present is significant because it creates consequences for the future.

When some trigger compels action, how consciously you perform that action becomes important. If you do it unconsciously, that unconsciousness will generate an enormous amount of karma. And that is how karma perpetuates itself.

Take the human population as an example. The moment two people act, you have consequences. A man and a woman get together and may produce a child. This is a simple physical example of how actions breed consequences. But the consequences can be on many levels in terms of thoughts, emotions, ideas, opinions, and actions.

Here is where the idea of good karma becomes important. You can alter your future simply by performing the right kind of actions in the present. You can transform your future without any spiritual process, without any elevation in consciousness. When you perform the right actions today, a positive future is assured.

But if you become meditative, you go a step further. Every spiritual tradition has encouraged people to meditate for this reason. When you become meditative, you do not merely create positive karma, *you stop breeding karma altogether.* In all spiritual traditions, to become an ascetic means just this: you stop breeding karmic consequences.

Let me offer a personal example. As a guru, when I am conducting a spiritual program, I am in a particular mode. If I embrace everyone before me with tears of joy and inclusiveness, it will not breed any karmic consequences. But if I do the same thing only with one person whom I know well, that same embrace will create consequences. This is because the inclusive embrace has *no karmic substance* to it. It is absolutely conscious action.

This is why, at a program, I never focus on the faces I know well. If I choose to meet another's gaze, I always pick a totally unknown face to address. As soon as you focus on someone you know and talk to them, it can turn into an entangling process. It would breed consequences for them, for me, and for the entire situation.

However, if I am developing a project, I do, of course, talk to intimate groups of people. I know this will not breed any entangling consequences for them, because what we are evolving is not about them or me, but about a larger vision. This is not entanglement, because it is an all-inclusive involvement. There is nothing selective about it.

Look at it this way. If your actions are coming from memory, they will most certainly breed karma. We always say, therefore, that all human actions can be only of two kinds: those that destroy karma (*karma-nashana*) and those that breed karma (*karma-vriddhi*). As a guru, my business is to impart the technologies that promote the former.

So how you handle your Actionable Karma in the Present is very important. If you are not conscious about it, you may think you are being spiritual, but you may simply be spiraling into entanglement.

In modern-day terminology, you could see the unconscious mind as Accumulated Karma (sanchita); the subconscious mind as Allotted Karma (prarabdha); and your conscious mind as Actionable Karma in the Present (kriyamana). This is not entirely accurate, but in its most broad terms it is a useful way to understand the differences.

We now come to the other aspect of Allotted Karma. This is Actionable Karma in the Future (*agami karma*). Your unconscious action today (in terms of thought, emotion, or action) will lead to consequences that compel your actions tomorrow or a year later—or, some would say, even a lifetime later. In other words, no matter what you do, life will drive you into a place where you *have* to act.

If you borrow from a bank, for instance, or have a mortgage, your karma of tomorrow is determined by today's action. Similarly, if you have a child, you are committing yourself to at least a twenty-year project. You have to think about providing for the child, sending them to school, putting them through college, ensuring that they stand on their own feet. What you do or do not do tomorrow is not decided by a whim. A simple action breeds enormous consequences.

It is Actionable Karma in the Future that perpetuates the human cycles of compulsive action, leading to what the Indian spiritual tradition sees as cycles of birth and death. It propels human beings to return to the embodied state, time and again, in order to work out their karmic inheritance.

If you find the idea of future lifetimes problematic, do not be distracted by it at this stage. Nor is it essential to an understanding of karma. For the true yogi, *there is just one life*. Yesterday you may have been dressed in one way, and today you may be dressed in another! Life, however, stays unchanged.

If you handle your Actionable Karma in the Present *consciously*, you will not breed any compulsive Actionable Karma in the Future. That is the key to handling memory. Let me stress that there is nothing wrong with a bank loan, a mortgage, or a family. Indeed, the more complex your karmic memory is, the more varied and interesting your life becomes. But the aim is to enjoy the process of life, not be trapped by it. Hence the importance of eliminating all manner of *unconscious* karma. You do not want to accumulate any karma that will compel you to act compulsively in the future.

To continue with the earlier analogy, when conducting a program, I embrace everyone inclusively and choicelessly. I do not choose to favor one over the other. If I were selective, the spiritual transmission would not be as effective. It is the choicelessness of my action that makes it impactful.

The karmic trap is always *in the choosing*. Choice is the great human gift; freedom is the great human possibility. However, instead of choosing inclusively, most human beings choose selectively. Most choose on the basis of compulsive likes and dislikes, on the basis of attraction and aversion. But when your involvement is *absolute*—that is, inclusive—you are not operating out of past memory. This means there is no compulsion, no consequence, no entanglement, no choice, no friend, no foe. When you perform Actionable Karma in the Present like this, you breed no Actionable Karma in the Future whatsoever.

On the other hand, if you choose to involve yourself selectively, based on *past memory*, the consequence lives with you. You are breeding more memory, whether physical, emotional, or intellectual. You are creating karma that will compel you into situations where you have to act in the future.

Once you understand how the karmic mechanism works, you know a basic difference: between *involvement* and *entanglement*. Most people do not understand the fact that it is possible to be absolutely involved without getting entangled.

For instance, whether I meet a stranger or a friend, my interiority remains the same. My involvement is total. I may communicate and act differently, but internally I remain the same. My way of being remains unchanged, although what I do or say is relevant to the situation and the person. This breeds no karma.

When involvement is selective, you fall into the trap of entanglement. Here is the central problem: Selective involvement leads to suffering and karma; detachment leads to lifelessness.

But involvement need not come from a place of memory. It can be conscious. For most people, involvement springs from memory and is compulsive. Once memory enters, action is enslaving. Without memory, however, you can operate consciously. When your action is unsullied by past impressions, it is liberating.

From Being to Doing to Having

The human equation was always meant to be like this: to move from *being to doing to having*. This means we were never meant to act *in order to find fulfillment*. Fulfillment was seen as an inner condition. It could not be pursued externally. We act in order *to express our fulfillment, not to acquire it*. We act in order *to celebrate our inner completeness, not to pursue it*.

For most people, however, this simple equation is reversed.

Most people *do* in order to *be*. They act because they feel incomplete. Their action is prompted by a desire to acquire something or to enhance their identity in some way. This is the ancient hunter-gatherer impulse, which still endures in human beings. It is the need to act in order to *accumulate*—whether it is physical, emotional, or intellectual satisfaction. It is action impelled by a desire to augment themselves, to become more than what they are. They *act* in order to *have;* they *have* in order to *be.*

This is tragic.

Most people have already determined what they want to have. Therefore, their doing is invariably to acquire something. Someone wants to earn fame so they might get into the movies or write a book, for instance. Their identity is now film star or author. They identify with this label. It now determines their being. Similarly, someone else wants to acquire the status of sportsman or politician or businessman. People even go around calling themselves golfers. I play golf and write books and ride motorcycles, but I am not a golfer, an author, or a biker!

I am not *doing* in order to acquire an identity. The way I am is untouched by what I do. I am not a yogi because I teach yoga. It is not my activity that makes me a yogi. It is my being that makes me a yogi. *"Yogi" is a description of my inner condition, not my activity.*

When you live like this, who you are always communicates itself in its own subtle way to people. The fragrance of who you are always gets conveyed. People sense that I am operating from this place of inner freedom even if they don't understand how it works. Very young people come up to me and treat me like their contemporary, or even their close friend. They call me Sadhguru, but it is not a term of distant reverence; it is one of familiarity, of affection.

Now, if my talks were about quoting from a scripture, such friendship and affection would be impossible. Scripture means memory; memory means hierarchy. This hierarchy turns one thing into sacred, another into filthy. What we consider sacred becomes an authority; what comes from an authority becomes our truth. And this kind of truth renders us incapable, paradoxically, of ever experiencing real truth! We have reached a point today where authority has become the truth. But soon as we turn inward, we realize that truth is the only authority!

However profound it is, all that comes from memory spells karmic bondage. *I do not come from a place of karma, so I do not breed karma.* It is as simple as that. What I say comes from inner experience, from a state of *knowing*, not from previously acquired knowledge. This is *chitta*, content-less intelligence.

The one thing that human beings simultaneously suffer and cherish is memory. You try to acquire and freeze memory in order to acquire an identity; you are trying, therefore, to do in order to be. But neither your identity nor your memory is essentially about *you*.

Think about it.

When you are sitting in a café, drinking your cappuccino, you can enjoy only your four dollars' worth of coffee. Whether you have ten billion dollars in the bank is irrelevant. The money exists only in your memory. To carry money around in your memory means you are a creature of the past. If you base your future on your past, you are as good as dead!

And this is why faces around us are becoming so grave. The grave is, after all, the abode of the past! And that is karma, too: a habitat of the past. Your Actionable Karma in the Future ensures that your future is exactly like your past. When nothing new happens to you, it is time to Rest in Peace!

The Causes of Unease and Disease

Allotted Karma in most human beings has its own level of complexity. A large part of it is devoted to physical action. Other segments are devoted to thought, emotion, and meditativeness.

The problem of modern life is that most people's physical and emotional energy does not find full expression in a lifetime.

People in civilized society carry a great deal of unexpressed emotion within. Now, if emotions never find full expression, the energy can turn around and become deeply damaging to one's health and well-being. This accounts for the upswing of depression and mental illness across the world. It is said that one of every five Americans suffers from some form of psychological illness in a given year, and fifty percent will suffer a mental ailment at some point in their lives. A staggering statistic!

The problem is that civilized society regards the uninhibited expression of emotion as a sign of weakness or of lack of sophistication. The suppression can create untold havoc in the human system. I would say ninety percent of the people in the world never find full expression for their emotions. They are afraid of their love, their joy, their grief, everything. To laugh loudly is a problem: it is seen as non-genteel or unladylike. To cry loudly is a problem: it is seen as unrefined and indecorous. We have set up a deeply restrictive culture for ourselves.

Now, the major portion of your Allotted Karma is devoted to physical activity. The body remains the major source of identification for most people even today. So though the ratio varies from person to person, ninety-five percent of the time Allotted Karma is oriented toward external action.

However, the level of activity in modern life has decreased drastically because people do not use their body the way they used to. If this unused energy remains dormant in the system, it could easily cause disease. The modern mind is going through a unique kind of neurosis for this reason. When you involve yourself intensely in physical activity, you expend a great deal of nervous energy. But now that human beings have become so inactive, almost every person suffers from some kind of anxiety or unease. This is simply because of trapped physical energy. In comparison, you will find that those committed to some form of intense physical exercise are often at a different level of balance and peace and much less entangled in sexuality and other physical drives. This is because one aspect of the person has found full expression.

One fallout of inactivity is disease. Trapped energy can also cause physical restlessness and agitation, which accounts for the state of chronic unease and disquiet that plagues the modern individual. You will notice that the very way people sit and stand reveals an absence of ease. They may have brought a practiced gracefulness to their movements. But the unease remains. If you take away the unease in your movement, it shifts inward to another dimension, where it is easy for it to find expression. In other words, it will build into your energy. In time, this disquiet on the level of energy manifests as disease.

In the Isha Yoga Center, many seekers are put into such intense states of activity that one might wonder why those on the spiritual path are working twenty hours a day? In popular perception, spirituality means someone half dozing under a tree! This is far from the truth. The intense physical work at Isha is an integral part of the spiritual journey. I want these people to finish all their Allotted Karma in a certain period of time. It is impossible to perform physical activity without your thought, emotion, and energies being involved. The same activity can, of course, be performed with different levels of involvement. Those who work only for a livelihood often feel constrained and suffocated. But when you are deeply involved in your work on every level, you will find activity invigorates you; it does not exhaust you.

Once you expend this karma, there will be no need for compulsive action. After this, action will be by choice. When the

Allotted Karma has been worked out, you can ask a person to simply sit still and there will be no struggle. The body will comply effortlessly.

In the higher-level Isha programs, we put people through immense, body-breaking activity so that afterward they are able to sit without moving. Meditation now happens naturally. When energy allotted for physical activity remains unused in the system, you cannot meditate, because the energy will make you restless and ill at ease.

There are certainly other aspects to disease. Environmental factors, as well as karmic reasons—from genetic factors to personal karmic reasons—play a part in why energy functions in a certain way and causes disease. However, many people are ill because they are not handling their Allotted Karma sensibly.

One aspect of energy being used to a considerable extent in today's world is mental energy. However, the overuse of mental energy leads to lopsided development and the invariable advent of disease. Consider a country's national budget: A certain amount is allocated for education; a certain amount for industry; a certain percentage for agriculture, development, defense, and so on. But if all these are not being expended, the economy suffers. The same happens within the body.

Those who have led a complete life often reach a certain natural state of peace and balance when they age. As the Allotted Karma starts winding down, you may notice changes in elderly people. You may find that their sleep quota comes down, and when they do sleep, you might find that they sleep deeply. This could be a sign that the Allotted Karma is drawing to an end. The great karmic warehouse remains, but one installment has begun drawing to its close.

A word of caution: Deep sleep does not necessarily mean the

end of Allotted Karma, but in the elderly, it could be *one* of the possible indications. When one installment of karma is over, the inner turmoil recedes and a new serenity and equipoise descends.

Some accomplished practitioners may go beyond their Allotted Karma. This could give them a certain aura of peace. But they have still not transcended their Accumulated Karma. They have moved from the retail shop to the warehouse. But they still have plenty of karma in stock.

For the spiritual seeker, Allotted Karma can be seen as cream on the milk. It is the karma that has surfaced in this lifetime. If you boil the milk well, the cream can further increase. So the spiritual process is a way of cooking oneself sufficiently to pick up as much karma from your karmic warehouse as possible in this lifetime and deal with it while you are conscious and able-bodied.

The goal for every freedom seeker is the same: to attend to your karma *now* rather than wait for life to throw it at you.

SADHANA

If you are experiencing deep emotional stress, a simple practice is to remain as far as possible in a posture where your spine is erect. The lumber region in particular needs to be relaxed and stretched to activate the spine. If you are able to squat for lengths of time, this is particularly beneficial because the extension of the spine has a profound impact on psychological well-being.

A natural upsurge of energy will happen if you keep your feet together when you squat. But not many people can do this. So the next best option is to widen the distance between the feet when you squat, keeping your feet in line with your shoulders. Make sure your feet are firmly upon the ground.

This is not just an exercise. The spine is not merely a collection of bones. It is the very basis of communication and perception within the human system. Keeping it in optimal condition will not just revitalize and rejuvenate the body but will make a phenomenal difference in your mental and emotional life and the way you function.

There is a more comprehensive seven-step practice called the Yoga Namaskar, which is offered free of charge on the Sadhguru app (isha.sadhguru.org/app). This is a powerful process of activating and strengthening the spine and the muscles alongside it, so as one ages, the spinal system does not collapse and the nerves are not pinched. If there is already spinal damage, this is a good way to regenerate the spine and ensure all-around benefits for the entire body. This is also a more scientific approach to unblocking emotional impasses in the human system and promoting what we call chitta vritti nirodha—the liberation of consciousness from fluctuations and bottlenecks.

FIVE

How Did It All Begin?

SUTRA #5

Pure intelligence creates memory out of itself;
the rest of creation projects memory as intelligence.

Intelligence Invents Memory

So how did this self-perpetuating carousel begin? How did we get into this condition of servitude to a memory cycle we don't remember starting? What got it started in the first place?

It happened.

On a certain day, a factory inspector in Russia went into a factory, picked out a particular worker, and asked, "If you had a shot of vodka, do you think you could still work?"

The worker scratched his head. "I guess so."

Then the inspector asked, "If you had a double shot of vodka, could you still work?"

The worker thought about it and shrugged. "I think I can," he said.

The factory inspector persisted. "And if you had five shots of vodka, could you still work?"

The worker replied, "Hey, aren't I here?"

That is karma.

You have had a million shots of vodka! Now, it is just your forefathers living through you, repeating the same old theater of life—with the same cues, the same triggers, the same reactions—over and over again. Where are you in all this?

You are as impaired by karma as one would be by five shots of vodka. In such a state, the more activity you are required to handle, the greater the suffering for you. Even if this activity brings financial and social success, there is suffering. Why? Because you are driving under the influence!

What is the point of this repetition, you might ask? For the human being who seeks freedom, this is a natural question. If you want to become free of outside influence, if you don't want your long-dead great-grandfather or your mother to be pushing your buttons long after they are gone, you might wonder how to step out of the cycles.

Which brings up the inevitable questions, Why karma? Who started this cycle? What is the origin of memory? What is its source? How did the whole drama begin?

The many creation myths in the world have tried to address this question in a variety of ways. The yogic creation story is a scientific truth expressed in strikingly poetic imagery.

It tells us that it all started with a realm of infinite emptiness. This is a dimension that has no memory at all. It is pure intelligence. It has no form, no shape, no size, no color. It is, in fact, no-thing. And yet it exists. This is called *shi-va*—that which is not. It is the very basis of creation.

Now, the very birth of form—even if it is a wave or just a particle—necessitates memory. You did not emerge from nothing. It is from the template of your parents that you were created. This means that memory or karma is a prerequisite for form.

So how did the first form happen? How did it materialize without memory?

The yogic culture personifies a certain concept, infuses drama into it, and turns it into stories. The story mode enables it to speak of dimensions that are beyond the realm of logic. And so it personifies infinite emptiness. It turns Shi-va—"that which is not"—into Shiva, the divine being who is the source of all creation. And so the story begins.

It happened.

Shiva, the Lord of creation, was lying in his nascent state, devoid of any karma. Then an element of dynamism entered this emptiness. This was Shakti, the active aspect of emptiness.

She approached Shiva and began to play with him. The human imagination sees the first karma as a sexual act. And so, as she aroused him, he woke with a great roar. He now assumed the form of a linga—a primal ellipsoidal form. This, the yogic lore tells us, was the first form in all creation. And with that sexual act, we are told, the whole of creation began. The primordial sexual act between Shiva and Shakti ignited the void into a dynamic state of creation, maintenance, and destruction.

And thus there emerged the grand theater of the cosmos: time and space, name and form, birth and death.

Gradually, form began to perpetuate more form. Memory began to spawn more memory. The karmic cycle was set into motion.

Some physicists I have met agree that the Big Bang that began the universe could well have been a series of bangs. In an automobile, if you take off the manifold and start the engine, it would sound like a volley of bangs. But if you throttle up, the engine roars. So a series of bangs in close succession does, in fact, become a roar. And so the Big Bang of modern science and the Big Roar of the yogic lore are not so different! Physicists also say that the first form in creation was ellipsoidal, reinforcing the yogic perspective that has always seen the linga form as sacred.

Interestingly, scientific experiments today show that if you create an energy pattern outside a chamber in a vacuum state, virtual protons and virtual neutrons will begin to appear. That means, to put it simply, that something is taking form from nothing.

Now, for the birth of form, as we have said, memory is a prerequisite. It is only because of elemental, atomic, and evolutionary memory that a snake is different from a tree, for instance. So in order to produce the first form, *intelligence invents memory*. This means the first act of creation marks the birth of memory, of karma.

Not surprisingly, Shiva as a deity is considered to have no parentage, no ancestry, no past whatsoever. He is called *swayambhu,* self-created. Here is a major difference between the source of creation and the rest of creation: *the source of creation is pure intelligence that creates memory out of itself; the rest of creation projects memory as intelligence.*

That is an enormous difference with a wealth of implications.

Another creation myth—that of Adam and Eve—also suggests that the birth of memory-based knowledge is the beginning of the Fall. It is with knowledge that Adam and Eve fell from Paradise. It is with knowledge, one might say, that the trap begins. Human beings now moved from a pristine intelligence to memory that projects itself as intelligence. They journeyed from intelligence to intellect, and from consciousness to self-consciousness.

What we call knowledge refers to frozen, accumulated memory. Knowing, on the other hand, is a dynamic process; it is living wisdom, not dead information. Instead of tending to the root, Adam and Eve grew fascinated by the fruit. Instead of nourishing the tree of life, they began to fixate on the succulence of the end product. They began choosing product over process, destination over journey, karma over yoga, knowledge over knowing. They were so beguiled by the consequences of their actions that they began to see life as a means to an end.

This is a sadly reductive way to live life. For as soon as you seek to freeze or grasp or manipulate the great roaring cascade of life, you have to stand apart from it. *The moment you stand apart, you create divisions: between root, stem, and fruit; between past, present, and future.* Now you have the birth of time. And with this, bondage begins.

In the East, we would see the Fall as the birth of cycles, the beginning of karma. We called these repetitive cycles *samsara*. The birth of memory is the beginning of form, of cycles of birth and death. And yet, in the East, we see this as neither good nor bad. It is simply the way things are when viewed from a limited perspective.

When cyclical time is born, memory becomes important. How a proton, neutron, and electron behave in a hydrogen atom is not the same as the way they behave in an oxygen atom. As atomic memory grows more complex, you have more names for all these atomic constructions, but in reality, these are just the different behaviors of the same particles. From the particle to the atom, from the molecule to the amoeba, from the fish to the human being, the differences are many, but, essentially, this process means an increase in the complexity of memory.

Look at the utterly staggering diversity of creation—all made possible by the capacity of a primordial intelligence to create memory!

Authentic Intelligence Versus Artificial Intelligence

At the age of thirteen, when I first saw a calculator, I was deeply offended. I wondered why on earth I was being tortured in my math class when all the teacher needed to do was to consult a machine for the answer! I dreamt of the day when there would be a machine for my science class and every other class as well.

In the world today, those with great memories are considered intelligent. They pass examinations with ease, often get the top grades, go on to get PhDs, and become scholars of repute. All this is, quite simply, because they remember what they study and are efficient at processing it.

In the yogic traditions, it is only if you touch chitta—the dimension of intelligence unsullied by even an iota of memory— that you are considered enlightened. Until then, you may be learned, you may be scholarly, you may know a great deal about creation, but you know nothing about the *source* of creation. You know nothing about the dimension of intelligence beyond the ambit of your personal karma.

Traditionally, in the Indian subcontinent, wisdom was prized over knowledge. Human memory was certainly valued, and those who could recite the Vedas backward were considered great scholars. However, thought was never accorded ultimate importance, because it was seen as the product of memory, of intellect. This is why the guru was considered more significant than the scholar. Education, parentage, and pedigree were socially significant, but never existentially significant. What was valued was this profound innate intelligence—a capacity to perceive existence as it is, rather than as we think it is or should be.

In the next couple of decades, the upswing of artificial intelligence will radically change the way we look at the concept of intelligence. Our ideas of education will be fundamentally altered. If you are looking for tools of self-transformation, a memory-based educational system will be of little use. The intellect, which is based on memory, is a wonderful tool. However, *it can only inform; it cannot transform.*

In an age of artificial intelligence, only those who are capable of exercising intelligence beyond memory will have something truly valuable to contribute. The fundamental difference between a human being and a machine is perception. Perception is something a machine will never possess. The machine will be capable of data accumulation, analysis, and action (all of which are functions of the intellect), but little else.

The human being is an organic machine, but a machine nonetheless. If we are to distinguish ourselves from other machines in any meaningful way, and not merely replicate their functions, we need to empower our capacity to perceive. For this, we need to reclaim our access to that unfettered unprejudiced intelligence—which in Sanskrit is called *chitta*—that is the basis of our lives.

What is chitta? It is the deepest level of the mind. It is awareness, aliveness, a profound intelligence that lies beyond intellect, beyond memory, beyond judgment, beyond karma, beyond all divisions. It is the intelligence of existence itself, *the living mind of the cosmos.* In the yogic tradition, it is said that once you distance yourself from the compulsions of your karmic software, as well as the identifications of your intellect, you are in touch with this unclouded consciousness. And only when we access chitta is self-transformation possible.

This is why, as a guru, I never bless people with the wish that their dreams should come true. Since dreams are simply based on memory, you can dream only of a more magnified and more improved version of what you already know! If your dreams come true, there is nothing terribly special about that. My wish is that your dreams should be *shattered*. Only then will something larger than memory manifest in your life.

May something you could never dream of happen to you.

Is Karma a Dirty Word?

We have looked at how karma began. Part Two of this book will look at how it might end.

But a crucial question we need to address is this: Do we really *want* it to end?

Is memory a burden? Is karma an obstacle? Is samsara a curse? Is life unmitigated suffering?

Not in the least.

Let me state this unequivocally: karma is *not* a dirty word.

Certain religious strains have, over time, begun to view the human being as inherently impure or soiled or sinful. They see human life as a curse rather than a blessing—a condition from which one needs to be cured or saved or rescued.

While freedom is a laudable aspiration, let us never forget this fact: *karma is the basis of human life*. Karma is what gives your physical form and psychological structure solidity and stability. It offers a foundation for your life. Without this foundation, there would be no possibility of transcendence. You, your body, and your mind are bound together only because of the karmic process. Without karma, neither your body nor your mind would exist. "You," as you understand yourself, would not be around!

So karma is, in fact, a tremendous possibility.

Every moment, impressions are flooding in torrents into your system through your five sense organs, and each impression is being recorded. There is nothing wrong with this. This stored information is very useful for your survival. If you deleted all of it, you would not know how to handle even the simplest aspects of life. Karma is the glue that makes you stick to this body-mind mechanism. If you washed away all your karma, you would exit your body this very instant!

Your software is not the problem. It turns into a problem only if it becomes the ruling factor in your life. Karma is just your own creation. It is neither virtuous nor evil, good nor bad. It is because you are looking at it through the prism—or prejudice—of memory that something seems wonderful and something seems horrible. Karma is the basis of your individuality, but it is also the basis of your prejudice.

The problem with karmic memory is that *it has stuck to you.* If everything that passes by sticks to this mirror, it is a no-good mirror. Your mirror can no longer show you life the way it is. Your perception is now seriously clouded. Now karma becomes a limitation.

Of course, there is much to celebrate about memory. Memory makes us unique. Memory makes every individual dazzlingly singular. It is responsible for the biodiversity and cultural variety we see around us today. It is memory that makes the world such an incredibly interesting place to live in. Memory is undeniably a privilege. An enormous privilege.

The rub is that memory is not just a glue. It is also a *boundary.* It offers you form and definition, but over time, that very form becomes a limitation, and the definition becomes a wall.

You are gradually fettered by the definitions you seek to acquire. You joyfully celebrate these definitions—perhaps of family, clan, tribe, class, gender, religion, culture, language—but over time these definitions harden into rigid markers of identity. Before you know it, you have crafted your own prison. Whether gilded or iron barred, a cage is still a cage.

The tragedy is that you are imprisoned by walls of *your own making*. These are walls and bars you have erected unconsciously, and which now do not allow you to escape. You are the builder, but you have now imprisoned yourself in your own home. Your creation that was a source of sanctuary and identity has now turned into a carapace. You have spun such a cocoon of confinement around yourself that now you cannot fly free. You have become your own jailer.

What then, is the way out?

Part Two of this book explores the various ways in which you can work with, and through, your karma to address this unquenchable human longing to be free. It offers you ways to enjoy memory without being oppressed by it. It offers you ways in which you can live in this world without adding to your already-burdensome freight of karma. It offers you a chance to navigate your journey through this world without being worn and abraded by the ride.

You can feel the breeze on your face and the sun on your skin, but you don't gather needless grime and aren't at the mercy of changing weather. The next section empowers you to make the journey homeward by showing you a path that the greatest sages have known since time immemorial: how you can be *in* the world but not *of* it.

This path reminds you that while karma is your bondage, if you handle it right, karma can also be a stepping-stone to your liberation.

PART TWO

◆

◇◇◇

A Note to the Reader

Yoga—literally, union—refers essentially to a science of transformation. If Part One of this book focused on the building blocks of karma, Part Two trains the spotlight on the technologies of transforming karma. It introduces you to the basics of *karma yoga*—the science of transforming memory into choice, passivity into dynamism, identity into possibility, sleepwalking into awakening.

Human conditioning, as we have seen, runs deep on the levels of body, mind, and energy. Merely addressing karma on one level—the mental or physical to the exclusion of the rest, for instance—will not work beyond a point. The swiftest and most effective path to joy and freedom is to address karma on *all three levels*—the physical, the psychological, and the energetic.

While Part One addressed the *what* of karma, Part Two is for those who want to address the *how*. It is for those who want to know how to decondition the body; how to rewrite the repetitive and unoriginal life narratives authored by the mind;

how to conquer the unconscious blocks and uncontrolled oscillations in the energy system in order to harness its transformative potential.

This book is about demystifying concepts, but not about denying them their mystery. It is about peeling away needless arcana. But it is not about oversimplifying complex truths. So if the discussion around the energy section begins to seem esoteric in parts, let that not dishearten you. Think of it as a reminder of the complexity of the yogic science—a complexity that is within your grasp, too, the deeper you delve into the subject.

Karma yoga works in three ways: It is a means to generate good karma for oneself. It offers a way to distance oneself from the oppressive aspects of one's karmic inheritance. And it is a means of shedding karma and moving toward one's ultimate liberation from cyclical existence. All these three possibilities are available to the karma yogi, the committed practitioner of the alchemy of well-being.

The approach here is more practical than in Part One. This explains the many Sadhana segments you will encounter along the way. However, let me reiterate that yoga is too subtle and refined a system to be imparted in words alone. It is a system that requires trained teachers, a controlled environment, and a high level of discipline on the part of the student. This part of the book can never be a substitute for a yogic initiation. However, it does offer several possibilities for self-experiment that can get even the uninitiated started on a journey of freedom and discovery.

SIX

Karma Yoga

SUTRA #6

In losing awareness of self is the trap of karma.
The hunter becomes the hunted, the architect becomes the
bonded laborer, the creator becomes creation.
A spider trapped in a web of its own making is a tragedy.

The Crippled Fox and the Generous Lion

It happened.

On a certain day, a man was seized by a spiritual thirst. In those days, when you were spiritually thirsty, you went to the forest. (Today, of course, that would be difficult, given that there isn't much forest around!)

So this man went deep into a nearby forest and found a tree, under which he sat cross-legged and began intoning the sacred syllable *aum*.

Now, you can do *aum* for only so long. After that, the stomach has its own *aum*, which asserts itself periodically! Each time his stomach growled, the man would go to town for a meal. He would then come back and resume his austerities.

One day, he returned after his meal and sat down on a rock. He was about to resume his chanting when he noticed a fox. It had lost both its forelegs but was still well-fed and healthy. This struck the man as distinctly odd. In a jungle, governed by the law of the survival of the fittest, it was strange to find a disabled but healthy animal. How had this fox managed to survive?

The man looked at it with some surprise. After a while, he resumed his practices.

That evening, while meditating, he heard the growl of a lion. He promptly forgot his *aum* and clambered up a tree.

A lion came by with a large chunk of meat in its mouth. To the man's amazement, the lion walked up to the crippled fox, dropped it in front of him, and walked away. The fox began tucking into his dinner.

The man looked on in disbelief. The same practice went on day after day. The man could not believe his eyes. A crippled fox being fed by a generous lion! This was a miracle.

"This has to be a message from God," he thought. "What is God trying to tell me?" He struggled with that question for a while, and then it dawned on him. When even a crippled fox was being fed in the jungle by a generous lion, why should he keep running to town in search of food? Surely God wanted him to trust he would be provided for and wanted him to focus on what really counted—his spiritual practice.

So the man changed his strategy. For the next three days, he kept up his *aum* practice without stirring from his spot. By the fourth day, he was considerably weakened; by the fifth day, he could barely stay conscious; by the seventh day, he was gasping for life, caught in the throes of death.

A yogi happened to be passing this way. Hearing these noises, he found the man and asked, "What happened to you? Why are you in this condition?"

"Because a divine message came to me. I obeyed it, and see my plight!" groaned the man.

"What divine message?"

And so the man related to the yogi the entire story of the crippled fox and the generous lion. "So tell me, yogi," gasped the man, "was this a divine message or not?"

The yogi said, "Yes, of course this was a divine message. But why did you choose to imitate a crippled fox rather than a generous lion?"

And this is exactly what we have done to our understanding of karma!

We have always had a choice: between inclusive action and paralyzed volition, between intelligent dynamism and pathetic fatalism. Why do we so often choose the latter?

When we say "Our life is our karma," it means that our life is of our making. What incredible freedom this spells! And yet what devious ways we have found to absolve ourselves of that responsibility. The moment we absolve ourselves of responsibility, our life resembles that of the crippled fox rather than that of the generous lion.

In most cultures of the world, people have been told that God determines the course of their life. They must therefore look up to God. But in the East, we said there is nothing to look up to. In a round planet that is spinning, what is *up* anyway? Your karma was created by you, and it is knowingly or unknowingly being created by you every moment of your life. Karma is, therefore, an invitation to look *within,* not upward.

Once you understand that you are a hundred percent responsible for your life, you will naturally choose to live consciously, rather than unconsciously. An unconscious life seems to be easy because you don't have to *do* anything other than live by your patterns and compulsions. But an unconscious life will not unfold the way you want it to. It is at the mercy of the caprices of your compulsions. A conscious life, on the other hand, will unfold in the best possible way for you.

Most people live in states of great inner tumult because they believe a God up there or others around them are responsible for their lives. However, the moment you see "My ability to respond is limitless," things settle. You have now shifted the source of creation from heaven to within. Now it doesn't matter whether you have confirmed tickets to heaven. Once you know the source of life is throbbing within you, those tickets are quite irrelevant!

The significance of karma is that it means that none of your identities—derived from beliefs, ideologies, religions, and systems of morality—are absolute. All of them are capable of constant evolution.

Indeed, of all the crimes that human beings have committed against one another and every other creature, the idea of heaven is the worst of all, because the assumption is that life happens at its best elsewhere, not here and now. Karma means that you are capable of being at your best and doing your best *in this very lifetime.* It implies a movement toward your ultimate well-being. It means you are capable of being in heaven, in the lap of the divine within yourself, *right now.*

Now you may ask, If karma means taking complete responsibility, what is grace? What is the role of the divine in our lives? Is karma a denial of God?

No, it is not. Let us look at this closely. What do we mean when we use the word *divine?*

By the divine we mean the source of creation.

Where is this source?

Within you.

Only because you *are* life are you capable of wondering about the source of life.

So the question is, Are you going to rest content knowing only the skin, flesh, and bone that make up your physical form, or are you going to seek the very source of creation within you?

If you know only the physical, you will live in a particular way. If you know the mental and emotional dimensions of your life, you will live a deeper life. But if you touch the very source of life, you are available to grace. Your entire life becomes divine.

Walking Alone

The one thing every seeker needs to remember is that the inner journey can only be undertaken alone. Once this realization dawns, it marks the birth of spirituality. This realization is sometimes scary for those who are used to living in groups, to making collective life decisions. Yes, you can walk together in the outside world, but in the inner world, everybody walks alone.

It happened.

A yogi was walking through the forest. He was suddenly accosted by a highway robber. This was a notorious robber with a reputation for looting and murder.

He was about to strike the yogi when the yogi asked, "Why are you accumulating these terrible karmas? What for?"

"I have to support my family," said the robber. "I am responsible for my wife, my children, my old parents. I have to kill you."

"If you are doing this for their sake," said the yogi, "it is also time you found out if somebody is willing to carry the burden of your karma. Please go home and find out. Tie me up to this tree, so I cannot escape. Just go home and find out for yourself who is willing to carry your karma."

So the highway robber went home. He said to his family, "I support you by killing people and looting them daily. Will you support me by sharing my karma?"

His father said, "Nothing doing! I am your old father; it is your business to take care of me. How you take care of me is your karma."

He went to his mother. She said the same thing. He went to his wife and children. They said the same thing. "It is your duty to take care of us. How you take care of us is your problem. Why would we share the karma of a murderer?"

Disillusioned, the man came to the yogi and fell at his feet. "You were right. Everyone is willing to partake of the rewards of my karma. But no one is willing to share responsibility for the adverse consequences of my actions."

Karma cannot be distributed democratically. While there is a dimension of collective karma—or kula vedana—there is also the Allotted Karma that every person has to work out. Whether it is worked out with meditation or love, with awareness or ecstasy, doesn't matter. The realm of individual responsibility exists, and it cannot be evaded.

It is true that separateness or individuality is fundamentally a myth. However, as long as a person is invested in this myth, the karmic bondage remains. The greater the investment, the greater the karmic bondage. In moments of great devotion, however, when the level of investment is low and an individual's personality has almost dissolved, it is possible for the veil of karma to be lifted.

It is said that when saints like Jesus and Guru Nanak (the founder of Sikhism), Buddhist masters, and innumerable yogis walked the earth, people were cured of their ailments just by touching their garment. An enlightened master can certainly create the possibility for a person's karma to dissolve faster. What would happen in a hundred lifetimes could be worked out in a few minutes. The presence of these masters could, therefore, have created an opportunity for these afflicted people's karmas to dissolve more swiftly. It is also possible on rare occasions for a master to take on an individual's karma, but most of the time the karmic allotment—even if put on fast-forward—still has to be worked out by the individual.

As long as you consider yourself to be an individual, you cannot pass the buck. Your karmas are your own.

The Way Out of the Karmic Web

As we have seen earlier, the yogic system tells us that every human being is composed of five bodies: the physical body, the mental body, the energy body, the etheric body, and the bliss body. Karma is primarily imprinted on the first three levels. If we address the first three levels, we can attain a state of extraordinary freedom from the karmic labyrinth.

Many people speak of freedom, but have no clue that they are getting more and more deeply entrapped in their own karmic maze. Despite being gifted with phenomenal levels of intelligence, they have forgotten the way out of this self-created web.

In losing awareness of self is the trap of karma. The hunter becomes the hunted, the architect becomes the bonded laborer, the creator becomes the creation. A spider trapped in a web of its own making is a tragedy!

It happened.

On a sunny afternoon, Shankaran Pillai decided to go fishing. He took a case of beer to drink because it was a particularly hot day. As he waited to get lucky, he started sipping beer. Fishing is a patience game, but most people don't know how to wait. As Shankaran Pillai waited, he consumed can after can of beer. The afternoon wore on. The hot sun and the beer made him drowsy.

All of a sudden, a big fish bit the bait and tugged at his fishing line. A drowsy Shankaran Pillai, who was sitting at the very edge of the riverbank, slipped and fell over into the water.

A small boy and his father were passing by. The little boy turned to his father and said, "Daddy, look! Is the man fishing the fish, or the fish manning the man?"

Look at your own life and answer this question as honestly as you can.

Are you running your own life, or is it running you?

You have pursued so much for your well-being: your home, your business, your car, your spouse, your child, your club membership. But look back now and see: have you caught the fish, or has the fish caught you?

It is time to stop the charade. There is only one way out of the spider's web. And it is the age-old journey from unawareness to awareness, from compulsion to consciousness. The journey known to the greatest yogis and mystics all over the world. The journey back to who you are.

The yogic tradition has long had a term for this: karma yoga.

Karma Yoga

What exactly is karma yoga?

It is the process of using your karma as a process to liberate yourself.

The logic of karma yoga is simple. Every single activity you engage in can be used as a process of entanglement or as a process of liberation. If your activity is used as a process of entanglement, it is karma. If you use the same activity as a process of liberation, it is karma yoga.

However, the misconceptions about karma yoga are many. A great many people use the term freely and erroneously. It is time to clear the many fallacies that have distorted human understanding and that have created over the years more confusion than clarity, more heat than light.

Let's start with the first misconception.

Many believe that karma yoga means unrelenting action. This is untrue.

Karma yoga is not about being busy. It is not about being in constant doer mode. It is instead about engaging in the kind of activity that frees you, about performing the kind of action that leads you to your own higher nature, toward your freedom.

There is also a widespread premise that karma yoga means social service; that a karma yogi is a do-gooder. This is yet another myth. Mere service is not karma yoga. Karma yoga has nothing to do with what type of action you perform, but rather *how* you do it. Even good deeds can be performed compulsively, rather than consciously. This can lead to entanglement rather than liberation. It is the *how* that makes the difference. It is the volition that counts.

If action creates bondage, it is karma. If action creates freedom, it is karma yoga. If you perform action miserably, it is karma. If you perform action joyfully and effortlessly, it is karma yoga.

It happened.

On a certain day, three men were working on a site. A passerby came and asked the first man, "What are you doing?"

The man looked up and said, "Hey, are you blind? Can't you see I'm cutting stone?"

The passerby went to the second man and asked the same question.

"What do you think I'm doing?" growled the second man. "I'm trying to earn my living. I need to fill my belly."

The passerby went to the third man and asked again, "What are you doing here?"

The man stood up in great joy. "I'm building a glorious temple!"

All three men were doing the same work. For the first man, his work was simply cutting stone. For the second, his work was simply a means to eke out a livelihood. For the third, his work was an opportunity to create something beautiful that he cared for deeply. The *how* is the pivotal issue.

Every single act in your life can be like this. It is not the *content* of your life that matters. It is the *context* of your life that does. So becoming a karma yogi *does not mean you have to give up whatever you are doing right now.* It means you do it with wholehearted involvement and, in the process, help create a more joyful world wherever you go.

The problem with today's world is that we have created rigid ideas of right and wrong. When our minds are so full of hierarchy, it is impossible to be wholeheartedly involved in any action.

When my daughter was twelve years of age, she came to me, a little troubled. I gave her just one guidance: "Never look up to anyone; never look down on anyone." If people practiced this simple sadhana, they would see everything just the way it is. If you look up to someone, you will exaggerate their positive qualities; if you look down on someone, you will exaggerate their negative qualities. But if you simply look—not for something, but just *look*—you will see things just as they are. Now your ability to navigate your way through life is greatly enhanced.

Have you ever walked on a level surface, expecting to find a step before you? The very expectation of a step makes you lose your balance! This is what it means to walk through life in a make-believe landscape that bears no relation to reality. Even if you're on flat land, you're out of balance!

The moment you say something is superior and something inferior, an entire mechanism of like and dislike, attachment and aversion, is set in motion. But when you see things with a certain inner equipoise, you will find an enhancement in every aspect of your life, whether it is managing a corporation or managing your family.

This brings us to the next fallacy about karma yoga. Karma yoga is usually interpreted as doing one's duty. This again is utterly false. Now, this may sound outrageous, but let me say it: *there should be no such thing as duty in this world.* Duty is tyranny. The very idea was concocted by people with vested interests.

Think about it. Every idea of duty comes from someone with an expectation. The rulers tell you what your duties should be toward them; the ruled tell the rulers what their duties should be toward them. Parents keep trying to remind children about their filial obligations; children keep trying to remind parents about their parental obligations. Husbands want wives to remember their spousal duties, and wives want husbands to remember theirs.

There is nothing as unbearable as someone doing something for you because they believe it is their duty. The sanctimony of it can make it intolerable. If you are too dutiful, you will die of its burden and people around you will die of boredom! If you have love for something, you do it; if you have no love, it is better to simply desist from action. *Doing something miserably or self-righteously is not a contribution to life.* When your activity is such suffering, you will create much suffering around you. If you can work joyfully, you should do it twenty-four hours of the day. If you cannot, it is better you stop. The planet is full of miserable people working hard and manufacturing more misery in the process, both for themselves and for everyone else.

The idea of duty comes from the ethical and moral systems

we have created in case our humanity fails. These are fallback systems. But as a guru, I want every individual's humanity to be active every moment of their lives, rather than work on a fallback system that mimics humanity but is actually a phony substitute.

If all the 7.8 billion people on this planet in 2021 grew very industrious all of a sudden, this planet would be finished in the next twenty years! Thankfully, fifty percent of the people are lazy. And it is that fifty percent who have saved the world! This is an unfortunate state of affairs. It should have been the intelligent and the active who are saving the world, rather than the other way around. But, regrettably, too many miserable duty-adherents are actually wrecking the world by being busy all the time!

Karma yoga is not a holier-than-thou adherence to duty. Instead, it is about making your entire life an *offering*. Only when action is performed like this does karma create no bondage. The world is full of people consciously trying to awaken love or spirituality in others in some way or the other. Most often this is done with great attachment to a self-image of being a compassionate or noble person. With such attachment, action is entangling. Only if there is a natural sense of offering can karma be elevating for the doer.

So the inevitable question is, *If duty is irrelevant, does it mean you can do whatever you want?*

Yes, it does!

But there is a caveat: whatever you do, there is a consequence. If you are willing to joyfully take the consequences of your action, go right ahead. But if you are going to cry over things when they turn unpleasant, it is best you regulate the action and act with some sensitivity and foresight.

Approaches to Karma Yoga: Awareness and Abandon

Karma can be shed in two ways: either by acting with awareness or by acting with total abandon. If you can do it with both, you are liberated. These are the two approaches to karma yoga. But without these two, everything that you do is an accumulation of karma.

Abandon is one of the most difficult qualities to find in the world today. The level of inhibition that people live with is truly amazing. It is responsible for several of the diseases—both physical and psychological—we see around us.

I often ask people, How many of you have grown up in families where you heard your parents laughing many times a day? Most of the time people are dead serious because they are burdened by this dreadful duty of having to bring up their children right.

Now, when large numbers of people grow up like this, exposed all the time to fear, anxiety, and tension, they naturally grow up inhibited. It may not be spelled out for them, but children pick up the fine print very easily: that it is not decent to laugh, to cry, to dance. In fact, what they imbibe is that it is not right to be *alive*! As adults, they believe that apart from going to an office, working all day, collecting their paycheck, coming home, reproducing, and struggling with their children, nothing else is appropriate.

Unfortunately, these inhibitions do not allow people to simply sit still. What no one realizes is that sitting still is one of life's greatest pleasures! If you can sit absolutely still, you will see that just breathing and being alive is the most extraordinary thing in the world. My schedule is a hectic one, but if I get the chance to shut my door and do nothing, that is the most wonderful time in my life. I have no need to read, watch television, or communicate with anyone, or to have even a single thought in my mind. The phenomenon of life is much larger than the phenomena of thought and emotion. When you truly experience life, your world of thoughts and emotions begins to seem puny and inconsequential. Just being alive is the greatest gift of all.

Even for one moment, if you are in deep embrace with creation, the source of creation is not far away. It becomes a living experience for you. But right now, you are not involved with creation; you are enamored of your own limited, self-manufactured creation, which is just a psychological projection. All your miseries, your tensions arise from this small make-believe world.

How, then, are we meant to live?

It is quite simple. Whether you walk or dance, work or play, cook or sing, just do it with total attention and awareness. Or else, do it with total abandon. Both ways, you are closer to creation. But if neither awareness nor abandon is part of your life, you are stuck in your own creation. This is a tragic way to live. When a creation of phenomenal exuberance and grandeur is around you, it is calamitous to live in your own cocoon of preoccupation. And the irony is, it is not even a cocoon entirely of your own making; it is molded by ten other people's opinions of you! Most people don't even know who *they* are, but they have opinions about everything else. You are allowing their opinions to dictate the nature of your very existence!

So what exactly do we mean by awareness?

First, let us remember that mental alertness is *not* awareness. Awareness has nothing to do with the logical mind. Nor is it what is commonly being referred to as mindfulness. Awareness emerges from the deepest layer of the human being. This is called *chitta*, or consciousness without content. Once you are in touch with this deepest layer, awareness happens effortlessly.

It happened.

Two priests were standing with a signboard that read: The End Is Near. Turn Around Before It Is Too Late.

A speeding car came along. The driver saw the sign, stuck his head out of the window, yelled "Leave us alone, you religious nuts," and sped on.

He turned the corner. The priests heard the hideous screech of tires and a huge crash.

One of the priests turned to the other and said, "Maybe we should just have the signboard read Bridge Is Out."

The problem with spirituality is that wrong signs have been shown to you for far too long. People have talked too much of mental awareness. There is no such thing. Mental alertness is not awareness. Mental alertness will help enhance your ability to survive in this world. The mind is a useful faculty of discernment, essential for survival, but of no existential consequence.

Awareness is a far deeper dimension. It is not something you do. It is not an action. It is a state of being. It is the way you are. Awareness is inclusiveness, a way of embracing this entire existence. You can set the right conditions for it to happen, but you cannot do it. If you bring the physical, mental, and energy bodies into alignment, there will be room for awareness to blossom. Once that blossoming becomes experiential for you, you explode into the oneness of existence. This is yoga, the ultimate union.

What about abandon? What does it mean?

It means that your involvement has become so intense that you are willing to abandon yourself. Most people think the word refers to abandoning someone or something! But this is about abandoning yourself. You are willing to just give up everything that you consider to be yourself.

Now, abandon can certainly happen by simply sitting still, but it is not easy. It takes great awareness to do this in a state of inaction. On the other hand, in intense states of activity—when you are running, dancing, or playing a game—you can give yourself up with total abandon. In such moments, there is a disconnect between your past and you. When you are completely lost or immersed in any activity, the influence of your past karma is no longer upon you. Many sportspersons and artists know this state of immersion, but the frustration is that they are unable to sustain it. Immersive activity can give you a taste of freedom, but it cannot last. Yoga is the science of sustaining that experience.

Many believe that a state of restlessness is a prerequisite for action. This is absolutely untrue. The paradox is that the basis of activity is in restfulness. Action that is born of restlessness is life-taking, not life-giving. It destroys a human being in the process. If action is performed in such a way that it is not about yourself anymore, you will see that your ability to work is almost limitless. You can be active almost twenty-four hours a day without exhaustion. This is the remarkable thing about karma yoga.

Now you may ask, What does all this have to do with being *spiritual?*

This brings us to yet another fallacy.

Being spiritual does not mean sitting under a tree half asleep! Being spiritual is not a disability; it is an empowerment. It does not mean limiting your sphere of activity; it means enhancing it. A spiritual person can cook, clean, walk, work, manage a business or a nation, do anything they want, and still be spiritual.

For such a person, their very life breath is a spiritual process. This could happen if their awareness rises beyond a certain level, if their love transcends certain limitations, if their physicality is very intense, or if the vibrancy of their energies goes beyond a certain level. A spiritual person is *one who has found action in inaction, and inaction in action*. Spirituality is about dynamism and stillness cohabiting within you to give you a taste of living death all the time.

SADHANA

A selective involvement is the basis of bondage and entanglement. Here is a simple sadhana toward your liberation. From this moment onward, be consciously involved with everything around you: the food you eat, the water you drink, the earth you walk upon, the air you breathe, the people around you. If you find this difficult, think of a person whose presence evokes the noblest and sweetest emotions within you. It could be a person living or dead; it could be Jesus or Buddha or anyone else you value most highly in your life. Then try looking upon everyone and everything around you with the same gaze. If this is hard to sustain, give yourself hourly reminders on your cell phone. A simple chant or mantra or tune could remind you of this. This will help establish you in the practice.

Be equally involved with everything without any distinction. Put away all hierarchies. If God comes before you, the same involvement; if a frog comes before you, the same involvement. (No, I am not talking of that frog that turns into a prince upon a kiss; just a frog!)

It may seem challenging at the start. But once you manage it, you will see that in just twenty-four hours you are capable of becoming an unimaginably blissful human being.

Renouncing the Fruit of One's Actions

When I was once asked what my mission in life was, I said, "Nothing. I'm just fooling around." My interlocutor was shocked. Fooling around? Was I being flippant? What did I mean?

And, yet, it is true. All my yoga programs, talks, conferences, and outreach projects don't mean a thing to me. Then why am I doing my damnedest to make sure people learn yoga and human well-being, you may ask? When I say it doesn't mean a thing to me, I am not saying it is useless. I know it is useful. I know this is what humanity needs right now. But personally, it does not mean anything to me. At the same time, I will do it as if my life depends on it—and if it costs me my life, I will still do it. My involvement is on at full throttle all the time.

Does this sound paradoxical? Actually, it is not. The problem is just that most people cannot do something unless they are personally invested in it. "This is the most important cause in the world," they think. Or "God has chosen me to do this work." People are always looking for their mission in life. What they never realize is that this is the way you build your karma! God has ordained no one. It is people themselves who build a false sense of self-importance by claiming that their work is divinely ordained. If they learned to plunge into something that does not mean anything to them with absolute involvement, they would find their karma disentangling in no time.

The basis of karma yoga is *to be involved in the process, not the product*. Whether you approach your karma through awareness or abandon, the point is to immerse oneself in the journey and not be anxious about the destination.

Start by looking at a practical example. Let us say someone is an accountant. The fact that they go to an office and count numbers does not in itself entangle them. But other reasons might impel them to work: the prestige of working in a particular firm, the financial benefits, the lifestyle it affords them, the social access it allows them. So gradually they might find they are no longer going to work because they love to count numbers, but because of the fruit of their actions. Of course, everyone deserves to be paid, to eat well, and to live well. But the question is this: If all those benefits were not there, would we still work with the same intensity and involvement?

You do not need to be a scriptural scholar to understand this. Just observe yourself. You will see that whenever you perform an action without expectation, your experience of life will be qualitatively different from the times when you perform it with expectation. A good example is to consider the times when you have played a game that you enjoyed. You plunged yourself into the game with passion and involvement, and of course you played to win, but you were not devastated if you lost. It is because you enjoyed the process that you were willing to play again. If you are very happy playing the game, the result does not really matter. If you are able to carry this awareness into every aspect of your life, your experience of life will be drastically altered. Above all, a game is won only when you play it well, not because you desire to win.

Since it is not easy for everyone to cultivate enough awareness to drop the fruit of their action, every culture in the world has emphasized the importance of love. When you have a deep sense of love toward somebody, it becomes much easier to drop the consequence of your action.

In this regard, women are definitely better karma yogis than men. Think of all the women who have worked quietly, tirelessly, anonymously down the centuries, without any prospect of financial reward or fame. Many of them worked full-time to look after their families, to make sure everyone was fed and clothed and loved, without thinking for a moment about what was in it for them. Unfortunately, we have devalued the contribution of these generations of unsung women.

Our current education has the effect of creating endless greed, unbridled want. Those who act without expectation of reward would be considered losers in the society we have created for ourselves. Our idea of progress is to want to be like someone else, or else to compete, to outdo others. This madness is the curse of our modern world.

Karma yoga reminds us that action is never a problem. It is the expectation of the fruit of the action that causes suffering. If you simply enjoy what you do and work at it wholeheartedly, there is no question of suffering at all. You would work joyfully, and your ability to work would be hugely enhanced.

Only a human being who is utterly blissful would be able to recommend renouncing the fruit of one's actions. When you are trying to attain happiness by hoping for a certain result from your activity, outside situations will determine whether you are joyful or miserable. This is why I am not impressed by those who endlessly quote the words of Krishna or Jesus or parrot Rama or the Buddha. Repeating a scriptural truth without an inner experience of it is a futile exercise. It will not transform your life in any way.

But a simple reversal of approach to your life can make all the difference. If you saw your life as an *expression* of your happiness, rather than as a pursuit of it, you would find you have made a significant paradigm shift. You would effortlessly immerse yourself in whatever you are doing, without any expectation, for the pure joy of the activity.

To Rule or to Serve?

Human beings have no choice but to act. That is the nature of our lives. But the two alternatives before us are just these: Do we want to rule or do we want to serve?

Now, I do not mean perform service in some self-conscious, holier-than-thou way. That is more an intensification of the ego than anything else. When I say *serve,* I mean an act of immersion, not conquest. Every human being wants to have an impact upon the world, but how you leave this impact is the moot point.

Do not think you are incapable of being a despot. Most people want to rule the world. It is just that because they are half-hearted that they end up ruling only their households! They may not have the capacity, the intensity, the one-pointed focus that is necessary to rule the world. But secretly they wish they could.

What makes a tyrant different is that their self-image is powerful. They might believe so strongly that they are going to rule the world that sometimes it almost comes true! This is something many human beings have yet to discover for themselves: that if they create a continuous mental focus toward a particular self-image, it will, in fact, come true.

There is, however, another way to create. It does not entail asking for anything, or even thinking about what needs to happen. Here, things just happen as they are needed. No forethought, no plotting or scheming is required here. Once you choose this approach, all you need to do is to act with tremendous intensity, without wavering for an instant in your focus and determination. Then, one day, you will reach a point where no action is needed. You are capable of acting, but you are not compelled to. You choose to engage with life, but you are no longer entangled by it.

This kind of action is possible for everyone. But before you arrive at this state, some fired-up action is required. People who have never been on fire will never know the coolness of water. People who have just lived their lives in a lukewarm, half-hearted, sedate manner can never reach a point of transformation. Those who have never known intense action will never be able to move into inaction. Their inaction will simply be lethargy, apathy.

Only the person who is capable of being immersed in work knows the true meaning of rest. This is why at the Isha Centers, as I have said before, you will find many residents engaged in unstinting nonstop work. They are not working at something they enjoy or dislike; they are not working to achieve something; it is simply single-minded, choiceless activity. They are doing it because it is needed, that's all.

You will see after rigorous, immersive work that there is suddenly no intention left in you to do anything. Now the real spiritual process unfolds. Only if you have known intense action will you know the bliss of inaction. Once your energies get to a boiling point, it is very easy to transform them and make your life happen in the most harmonious way possible. That is the whole purpose of karma yoga.

This is also the science of creating a truly powerful being. This is how one who serves is created. Their power is immense, but it is not the power to rule. The power to rule is not a real power, because it can be taken away at any moment. The power that we are talking about here is a power that cannot be taken away. In whatever circumstance or context such a person is placed, there is only one thing they will do.

Those who seek to rule can work only if they are on their throne. If they are taken off the seat, they become miserable. But those who choose to serve will be undeterred because they are not obsessed with the fruit of their action. If they are in heaven, they will do the same thing; if they are in hell, they will do the same thing. According to Buddhist lore, Gautama the Buddha said he would rather serve in hell than go to heaven because, anyway, he was incapable of suffering. That was his freedom.

This approach releases you from attachment to the fruit of your action. Now the action will happen by itself; it will also dissolve and melt away by itself. You do not have to stop working to be liberated from action; it will happen anyway. You do not have to do anything about it.

It happened.

In a Zen monastery, there lived a master who was more than eighty years old. Every day, he worked his heart out in the gardens—a time-honored part of Zen spiritual practice. He had been doing this for years. Now he had grown old and weak, but he refused to stop his work.

His disciples tried to dissuade him. "Don't bother with this anymore, Master," they said. "We are all here. We will do it."

But the old master wouldn't listen. His physical abilities had weakened, but the intensity remained the same.

So one day his disciples took away his gardening tools and hid them somewhere. He hunted for them in vain. That day he did not eat. The next day, again, his tools were missing, so he did not eat. The third day, no tools once more. He did not eat.

Now his disciples grew afraid at his refusal to eat. The next day, they replaced the tools in the gardening shed. That day, the old monk worked and ate. In the evening, he gave his teaching: "No work, no food." And that night he died. The four days of fasting had weakened him considerably. But his teaching was succinct, and he delivered it before he died: no work, no food.

Now, wherever you put such a man—heaven or hell—his action will remain the same. When you are like this, you are released from the vagaries of the external situation, from the cycles of karma. Merely closing your eyes won't achieve this. Merely running away and sitting in the mountains won't achieve this. The moment you open your eyes, the moment you return to the marketplace, reality will come and catch up with you. Karma has to be worked out, but engaging with action with great involvement and intensity, without caring a hoot for it, is the most effective way to work your karma out.

There are various ways to do so. You could be so drunk with blissfulness that nothing matters, or you could fall so deeply in love with someone that nothing matters. Only if you are in states of bliss or love can you work intensely and still not be bothered about the result.

The Meaning of Sacrifice

The term *karma yoga* is often seen as closely linked with sacrifice. In every spiritual tradition in the world, the notion of sacrifice has been seen as significant.

In Sanskrit the word *yagna* is often translated in English as "sacrifice." But *yagna* usually refers, in practice, to certain oblations and rituals that were practiced in ancient India to appease a deity or to placate some forces of nature. However, these rituals were not a sacrifice in the true sense of the word. *Giving up something for something else is commerce; giving up something for nothing is a sacrifice.*

The traditional yagna had its own technology and internal logic. It was a process through which you found access to certain forces or deities and sought to enhance your capabilities. These processes are still practiced today in many parts of India. They can help create several health and material benefits.

However, once you are on a spiritual path, you are not interested in small processes, minor technologies, petty rituals. The very way you live becomes a yagna. This is the deepest meaning of sacrifice. You are not interested in inviting an expert to perform rituals to enable you to manipulate certain forces. Your very life process is an offering.

If even a small percentage of the world's population becomes meditative, many reap the benefits. A single mango tree can offer fruit to a hundred people. Similarly, when your life becomes a yagna, thousands of people can reap its benefits. Many individuals have done this down the ages.

At Isha, there are thousands of volunteers and practitioners who have offered their entire lives to a spiritual path with commitment and unwavering focus. Wherever they go, they transform the place, in their own small way, into a *yagna bhoomi*—a land of sacrifice.

Do not think of sacrifice as cheerless self-denial. When one's entire life becomes an offering, it brings its own unique joy. There is a story about an Indian ascetic who went to the United States in the last century. Someone he met there dismissively commented, "As an ascetic, you know nothing about life; you have not tasted wine or slept with a woman. What can you know of life's experiences?"

The ascetic calmly replied, "I come from a land of sacrifice. And I know the bliss of sacrifice far exceeds the pleasures of the world. I am not afraid of your pleasures, and I am not denying or denouncing them. But once you taste a deeper joy, these become childish toys, mere sops, minor distractions."

This approach was at one time deeply ingrained in the Indian family. It was not perpetuated as a teaching, but as an everyday practice. It was part of the spiritual culture. In a host of different ways, a child grew up observing that the more deeply fulfilling life was about giving, not taking; about serving, not ruling.

My mother, like so many other mothers, was a prime example of this. She never had to say to us "I love you," because it was
so apparent in everything she did. Every morning, after ensuring
that her family had eaten, she would take a part of her breakfast
and go to the backyard. Here she would feed the ants that lived
there. She would never eat without feeding them. Today, modern families would be spraying the backyard with pesticide! But
without any self-conscious ecological mission, it was clear to my
mother that the ants had as much right to this planet as she had.
Every little action in her life had become a yagna.

For people whose lives have become like this, there is no
need to perform any ritual. Their lives have become an expression of love—not love as "I love you" and "you love me," but as a
basic ambience of their interiority. Now their lives are one ceaseless flow of karma yoga, an endless outpouring of their inner joy.
No more is needed.

SEVEN

Karma Yoga and the Physical Body

SUTRA #7

If you take more karmic load now, when you are well and capable, later you will walk "hands-free"!

"Embodying" Karma

Let us look at how karma yoga can be practiced on the level of the very first dimension of the self that we are aware of: the physical body. How is the physical body influenced by karmic memory? And how can we use the physical body to be free of the cyclical bondage of karma?

There are many imperceptible ways in which the karmic structure influences and even distorts the physical body. It is not merely your lifestyle—what you eat, what you drink, what you inhale—that has an impact on your body. The subtlest aspects of your thought and emotion can also influence the physical.

Start with a simple example. You can usually tell if a person is happy or despondent if you look at their face. If you become more observant, you will find that when disturbed, people actually sit or stand differently. Over time, these postures turn habitual and harden into vasanas, or tendencies.

Now, the mind does different things on different days. One day it is joyful; the next day, it is depressed; the third day, it is stressed. In the process, it is not merely distorting your vision of reality; it is distorting your body as well.

Think of all the unexpected things that happen on a daily basis that are not in your control. If every little psychological event were to reshape you, you can imagine what a complete distortion you would have become in a few years! The distortion will happen dramatically on an energy level, but it will take time to manifest physiologically.

If you look carefully at people who have gone through a certain level of emotional stress recently, you will notice small changes in their physical appearance. Often, if the left eye appears slightly smaller than the right, you can be quite certain that they have been going through some emotional distress in the past six months (unless, of course, they were born that way). This is because the left side of the body is always associated in yoga with the emotional life of the human being and the feminine dimension, symbolized by the moon with its cycles of waxing and waning.

Depending on the nature of the karmic memory, certain parts of the body also behave in certain ways. You might have noticed this about your own body: You may exercise as much as you can, but one muscle in your body is invariably less cooperative than the others. You may check it out with a doctor, or take an MRI. Both will most likely tell you that the muscle is perfectly fine. But your karmic inheritance shapes the skeletal system and musculature in very singular ways. Not every muscle is equally strong or capable.

Again, if you pay close attention to the body, you will see that in some parts of the physical system, you feel no sensation at all. In other words, there are blocks or gaps in the sensory process. This again is because the karma creates its own structure. Based on this karmic information, the physical body takes a particular shape.

Modern medicine is now well aware of the notion of psychosomatic ailment. This acknowledges the inseparability of the mental and physical bodies. As we have seen earlier, for every sensation, there is a mental fluctuation and a corresponding chemical reaction. The same process also works in reverse. Your physical structure, constitution, and general health are decided by this relentless process.

This is why yoga works so closely with posture, breath, attitude, and intention. If a certain awareness is brought into these aspects of the self, what is happening in the mind or in the outside world will not affect the body. When you are psychologically distraught, it is particularly important to hold your body consciously, because your karmic substance is trying to shape your body according to its distortions. This explains the enormous care brought into the practice of *asanas* and *pranayama* (physical postures and breathing processes) in yoga.

Karma Yoga and Asanas

How exactly does the physical dimension of yoga—hatha yoga, as it is called—prepare the body to deal with karma?

The logic is simple. If you cultivate the body in a certain way, it will actually be capable of taking on more of a karmic load.

This is how your Accumulated Karma (sanchita) transforms itself into Allotted Karma (prarabdha). The estimation of how much of a karmic load you can take on is done by your own innate intelligence. This intelligence will decide the volume of the stock you should handle for this lifetime, based on your physical and energetic capability and, of course, the karmic balance you have.

Certain cycles play out routinely in human life. Around every twelve years, a shift enables you to take on more of a karmic load. The first twelve-year cycle begins for a child somewhere between 54 and 108 months (that is, between four and nine years of age). Many human beings with a certain sensitivity to life are aware of subtle changes around the cusp of each twelve-year phase; these are times of greater receptivity and greater vulnerability, as well as increased possibility, times when changes in life direction often happen.

Certain shifts take place during every winter and summer solstice as well. Yogis have traditionally made use of these shifts to increase the amount of karma they can work out. Each cycle of the moon also marks a shift. Those who are into intense yogic sadhana often choose to take on an extra stock of karma on a new-moon day.

An Aesop's fable illustrates this point beautifully. Wherever a particular master traveled, his servants followed him, distributing all their luggage among them. Aesop always picked up the heaviest load although he was not a particularly strong man. All the others picked up the lightest loads, because the journey went on for several days. But he always carried the heaviest. One day, his fellow workers asked him, "Why are you doing this? You're a small fellow. Why are you choosing to carry the heaviest load?"

He replied, "I pick up the food bundles, which are the heaviest. But the thing about the food bundles is that with every meal, the load becomes less and less. And on the last two days, I walk empty-handed!"

Preparing the body is similar. Through yoga, you prepare the body to take on more of a karmic load. If you take more karmic load now, when you are well and capable, later you will walk "hands-free"! There is nothing to carry, and your life becomes beautiful. This is why the daily schedule in the Isha Yoga Center, as I pointed out earlier, is so rigorous. Physical activity here is intense so as to burn up the Allotted Karma as soon as possible.

As we know, each human being is born with different allotments of karma. These differences are sometimes apparent even in the mother's womb. As they grow up, each child is different. Based on this, the child's innate intelligence decides how much energy is to be allocated to different kinds of activity: physical, mental, emotional, and meditative.

Now, let us say someone has chosen forty percent for their physical activity, forty percent for their emotional activity, and ten percent each for their intellectual and meditative activity. As a result, they are likely to be a hyperactive mess! If someone like this comes to the center, I would put them into some intense physical activity for a few months. The idea is to burn up the energy allotted for physical activity in their Allotted (prarabdha) Karma. Only after this energy is burned up will they be able to sit quietly and meditate. Most people cannot sit still if they do not first go through some intense activity.

After that, life becomes much simpler. In any case, the life process itself burns up karma. Simply living and breathing destroys large volumes of it. So after this initial period of fired-up activity, things become easier, as long as people learn not to pick up a new load. In short, at the start, you pick up the heaviest load, but like the food bundle, you know it will go away! On the way, of course, you just make sure you don't go picking up garbage. The aim is to burn up your allotment, and then enjoy the delights of traveling light.

Common Karmic Frictions

People experience some common psychological frictions throughout their life—frictions that they call stress. Stress is caused when people try to run their life engine without adequate lubrication. However, some basic yogic practices can offer the needed lubrication for everyone's life.

There are more complex levels of friction when the karmic inheritance doesn't fit well with one's physical body—for instance, when a certain karmic inheritance does not find the right kind of womb. There are also times when the energy body does not fit well into the physical body. (For some reason, I see more such people in the east coast of America than in the west, or in the northern part of India than in the south. This might be connected to the nature of the land itself, the kind of memory the geography carries, the general atmosphere, or various historical factors.)

The practice of hatha yoga helps to knead the physical body as well as the entire system (including the karmic system) in a way that smoothes these frictions out. After sustained hatha yoga practice, when you simply sit, you feel no sense of discomfort or stress. Now you can sit still if you want to, as well as negotiate the outside world with great ease and capability.

Sometimes, because of education, technology, altered social situations, or a certain acquired competence, people are able to attain a state of well-being even though their current karmic situation does not allow it. They live lives that are way beyond their karmic blueprint. In short, they have been placed in far better life situations than their karma allows.

At such times, it is very important to upgrade oneself. Otherwise, you will end up suffering your well-being! This is a common malaise in the world today. Most people's problem is not a life that is hellish, but a life that is too heavenly! These are the ailments of privilege. People's systems grow confused because the information within them says one thing, but their life events say another.

There are ways to address this malaise. Learning to live in gratitude is extremely important because it creates the right attitude. It is also vital to keep upgrading one's software, as it were. Daily hatha yoga and kriya can help enormously to shed karmic burdens, to upgrade one's system and adjust one's software.

All these yogic sadhanas help one to maintain an inner state that is untouched by the outside. It does not matter whether you are in a palace or a hut: you are the same person. Wherever you are, you do the same thing. When you maintain this equanimity, you will see that situations around you keep getting better. But without karmic upgrading, old compulsions will overwhelm you. They will push you toward certain atmospheres and situations and will not permit you to come to terms with your new reality.

SADHANA

As we have seen earlier, karma builds itself on three fundamental levels: mental fluctuations, chemical reactions, and sensations. The sensory body is the outermost manifestation of the unconscious mind. The unconscious mind is ruled by an enormous library of karmic memory. This karmic memory keeps manifesting all the time without your permission. Since it is an unconscious manifestation, it makes you look like one big mess. But once you make it conscious, it could be very useful information.

Of the 114 chakras (energy centers) in the human system, the karmic substance concentrates itself around some specific ones. These are related to certain joints and nodes in the body. Chemical deposits build up here over time.

You may have tried mentally to alter certain simple habits, but you find that within a couple of days, you fall back into them. It is not easy to come out of karmic limitations without simultaneously addressing them on the chemical and physiological levels.

Hatha yoga is a way of shedding karma with full awareness by moving and stretching the body in various ways. This requires training, however. So here is a simple practice that allows you to move from outer to inner, from body to mind: from outermost sensation, to the chemical deposits within the body, to the mind with its fixed ways of thinking and acting.

Close your eyes. Raise your hand in front of you to the level of your face, and gently stretch the muscles in your hand, without necessarily moving it mechanically. You will notice lots of sensations. Watch the sensations as keenly as you can. Stretch the hand fully. Become aware of the twitch of every single muscle in your hand.

If you are able to notice the minutest sensations in your hand, you are ready to do this for the entire body. Continue to keep your eyes closed. Now stretch every muscle in the body and observe the sensations.

Do not turn this into a mechanical exercise. Allow

yourself to make it a subtle dance-like movement, very gently extending every fiber in your body and observing every sensation.

This simple process can help release chemical deposits in the body that have built up over time because of the many shifts and fluctuations in thought and emotion. This is one way of releasing them and, in the process, shedding karmic deposits as well. In the process, the very way you perceive and experience the world will be altered.

Additionally, this is a useful way to start cultivating awareness. Generally, people inhabit the body in unawareness. Only when they experience a toothache or a backache do they suddenly become aware of the body. The rest of the time, although the body is there, it is inhabited unconsciously. So one of the simplest ways to begin cultivating awareness is to start with physical awareness.

Awareness does not stop there; it deepens into various other dimensions. But starting with the body—which is a constant factor in your life—offers you an opportunity to practice maintaining your awareness continuously.

Karma and the Elements

We have seen in Part One how elemental memory plays a role in shaping the human being. Five elements make up the human system, the planet, the solar system, and the entire universe. Without them, there would be no creation.

With just five elements—earth, water, fire, air, and ether—think of the incredible diversity of life. We see millions and millions of manifestations around us, and no two individuals are ever the same. What makes this extraordinary diversity possible? It is the fact that the elements are highly receptive and have the capacity to acquire memory. Over time, a layer of information— or what we might call *karmic substance*—gathers on each of these elements. Without these layers of specific information, each human being would not be so utterly unique. The elements play a major role, therefore, in perpetuating karma.

Yoga has a system called *bhuta shuddhi*, which is about cleansing the elements of accumulated information or karmic substance. The five elements imbibe and hold information. This information naturally creates intention. Once you have an intention, you naturally start moving in a particular direction. By cleansing the elements of this layer of information, bhuta shuddhi is capable of transforming a human being in miraculous ways.

Every yogic practice—whether it is a posture (asana) or other hatha yoga practices, or a breathing process (pranayama), or kriya (internal action)—is actually a way of cleansing the elements within us. But there is also a direct bhuta shuddhi process that is a hugely powerful way to clean up. This cannot be taught in a book, because it is a process of transmission, not instruction. But it is important to introduce readers to the existence of this possibility, because it is one of the most effective processes of inner cleansing.

I believe I have initiated more women into the process than has ever happened in the past. Since the play of elements is different in the sexes—particularly fire and water, which are dominant in the female system—the traditional bhuta shuddhi process has been male oriented. However, by adapting it, we can make the same possibility available to both sexes. I believe this is necessary for our times, in order to ensure that no one is excluded from the amazing transformative potential of this process.

What makes this process significant is that, over time, the elements in your system will be in consonance with your intentions for life. They begin to function the way you want them to. Over time, this will also have some impact on the elements around you.

Eastern medicinal systems—including Ayurveda and Siddha—have always been based on the perception that no two human beings are alike. The way the elements function in one person is not the way they function in another. This makes them unique designer systems of medicine that are hard to standardize. The doctor prescribes differently for each person, because the treatment is based not on the ailment, but on the individual's constitution. Five different people with the same symptoms will be treated differently. A deep understanding of the elements underlies this.

Several human beings (not necessarily spiritual in any way) have found a way to perform bhuta shuddhi unconsciously. You may find people who are leaders in business or politics or art in the world who have this ability: when they enter a room, they change the atmosphere around them by their sheer presence. This is because of a certain amount of unconscious bhuta shuddhi. What is done unconsciously, however, has great power when done consciously. When bhuta shuddhi is done consciously, the elements rearrange the way they function within you in dramatic ways.

Bhuta shuddhi is actually the most fundamental level at which we can cleanse karma. People can decide to cleanse the mind one morning by trying to alter their attitudes, but by the afternoon they lapse back into old grooves of thinking. This is why yoga does not work solely with psychology. It is a known fact that the human mind is notoriously unstable and given to oscillation. Yoga places greater faith in the physical.

However, bhuta shuddhi is a way of addressing the very root of your karma—the patterns and predispositions that determine the person you think you are. If you prune the tree, it will sprout back with a vengeance. But if you dig out the root, it will be gone. So bhuta shuddhi is about radical transformation, not superficial change. It is about voluntarily relinquishing your compulsive hold on everything you have created—good, bad, ugly—so that the very source of creation can shine within you.

SADHANA

Human performance in any sphere is always gauged in comparison with someone else's. If your capacity to perceive is better than another's, you have a major advantage over them. For if you enhance your perceptual capability, or your ability to *see*, the effectiveness of your action will be greatly enhanced. I often tell seekers that the aim is not to see *something*, but to simply learn to see.

In order to enhance this perceptual ability, you could try a simple practice called the Akashi Mudra. You could do this practice particularly on those occasions when you feel you need to be at your best or to perform at your optimal capacity.

There is a point of convergence in your energetic body that stretches beyond the physical body. It is approximately seventeen to nineteen inches from the point between your eyebrows. You must search for the point where the vision meets at an acute angle of eleven degrees. Finding that point of convergence boosts the *akasha*, or etheric element, within you. The moment the element of akasha is dominant, you will find the clarity of your perception hugely enhanced.

Minimizing Physical Memory

In Part One, we looked at the insidious nature of physical memory, or runanubandha. Runanubandha is inevitable and vital for human survival, but, beyond a point, it can become a source of bondage. In a single lifetime, the volume of physical memory increases enormously. The reason is that people do not know how to manage and minimize the runanubandha in the system.

This is why traditions fixed a certain stability in norms and practices—whether in terms of having a single partner, or something as simple as not accepting food or water in a stranger's home, irrespective of their caste or class background. In traditional homes in India, people did not accept salt or lemon or sesame seeds from another's hands. These substances are particularly effective carriers of memory. The premise was that the body remembers any kind of intimacy—not only with another physical body but with any physical substance. Some substances were considered to be more effective conductors of memory than others. For the same reason, in the yogic system, those who are into certain practices were asked to apply sandalwood paste or turmeric on the body. Others smeared earth on their body; a few others, ash from the cremation grounds.

This is not mere ceremony and superstition. Today, forensic science has developed to the point that it is possible to tell through thermal imagery exactly who sat in a place seventy-two hours ago. The temperature of the body actually leaves a thermal imprint. Dogs have always been capable of tracking people down by picking up olfactory cues. Canine science is an old and advanced one!

Every touch actually imparts a karmic imprint. Most people are not aware of this, but this imprint remains on a subtle level. One of the most sensitive areas of the body is the hands. By touching hands, runanubandha is effectively transmitted from one person to another.

Holding hands is considered to be an intimate gesture for this reason. This simple act can bring two people even closer than sexual activity can. When sexuality is paramount, the need to explore the other's body will be paramount. When you feel really close to someone, it often feels adequate to simply sit and hold hands.

This is why the Indian tradition evolved the gesture of the *namaskar:* of folded hands in greeting when you meet someone, rather than kissing or embracing or shaking hands with them. The aim was not to clutter your system with too many physical connections.

The namaskar is a beautiful greeting because it is a deeply respectful acknowledgment of the source of creation within another person. If you look at a person's body or personality, you could either like or dislike it. This means a karmic pattern of craving or aversion is being set in motion. But when you bow down to the source of creation within someone—which is the same source that throbs within you—it means you acknowledge your shared and inherent divinity. You also ensure that you do not get entangled with yet another body through superfluous physical contact.

The practice of touching a guru's feet arose from the same understanding. Like the hands, the soles of the feet are particularly sensitive. By touching the feet, the guru's energy could be transmitted to the disciple. An entire science exists around how the guru's feet should be touched to ensure the maximum benefit. (Fortunately for me, most people do not really know the science! Although many Indians dive at my feet, they usually don't go beyond a token gesture.)

There are several other cleansing systems that make use of the purifying powers of the elements. In my own life, when I was into intense yogic practice, I would have somewhere between five to seven showers a day. When your system becomes so sensitive, you become conscious of the impact of every physical contact with your body—from a hand that you touch to the very cushion you lean against. Traditionally, yogis took a dip in the river at least twice a day at the very minimum. Flowing water can help erase runanubandha to a great extent.

Interestingly, Nature offers some natural ways to cleanse oneself of karmic cycles. At certain times of the year in parts of the northern hemisphere, for instance (July and December–January), the elements of air and water are particularly strong and fluid. This allows one to cleanse oneself effortlessly. Karmic cycles that have become entrenched can be dropped by simply allowing the external elements to work upon you. Here is effortless bhuta shuddhi that happens for free!

During certain times, simply standing in the wind can work wonders as a cleansing process. If you try standing in a strong wind for half an hour, you will soon learn what a proper "air wash" can achieve! It can leave you feeling so much lighter and rejuvenated.

These are times when grace is naturally on your side. Seizing this opportunity can be particularly beneficial for people who are stuck in small karmic cycles. This is the right time to break free of small habits or niggling irritants in your life and see each day as a wonderful opportunity to step into unfamiliar terrain.

Traditionally, fire was also used as a means of cleansing. The "fire wash" is used even today in many homes as a way of washing away negativity. These sensitivities developed because the entire tradition was oriented toward decluttering the system of the impressions gathered through random exposure to people, situations, and atmospheres.

Even today, in the Isha Yoga Center, the monks wash their clothes separately. Mixing up the clothes in a washing machine may be easier, but it is not done because each one is at a different level of spiritual attainment.

This is also the reason why the monks in the East traditionally wore earth colors. They use a very finely sieved red earth to wash their clothes, because this ensures that the only real runanubandha you hold is with the earth, not with the people around you. It is a tangible testimony to your connection with the planet: a reminder of where the body comes from and where it will eventually go.

The old songs and poems of the East, from the ancient love lyrics to pop songs in cinema, extolled lifetimes—*janam janam* (life after life)—of togetherness, not merely for romantic reasons. Continuity and stability were valorized because they ensured a firm and reliable basis to your life from which you could aspire to the ultimate. Marriage was not just about two people's little romance and their little families. It was about two people coming together for their ultimate liberation. This is why so many traditions view marriage as a sacrament. In traditional Hindu ritual, the mantras chanted while the couple circles the sacred fire is about consecrating the relationship and energy of two people so that they can both grow together to their ultimate possibility.

Today, at Isha, we are conducting what is known as the *bhuta shuddhi vivaha*. This is a marriage based on bringing about an elemental cohesiveness between two people. In a world where couples see relationships as more and more hard work—where love has become labor—this kind of marriage creates harmony on the most fundamental level possible, making it a more lubricated and graceful partnership.

When a certain stability in physical, genetic, emotional, and social relationships is attained, individual human life can grow to its peak. When there is instability, the physical memory grows confused and, over a period of time, can create serious psychological and physiological imbalances. If your ultimate aim is liberation, if your ultimate aspiration is to evolve into a divine possibility, this stability offers you an unwavering foundation from which you can extend yourself toward your final destination.

SADHANA

The physical world is a product of polarities: masculine and feminine, yin and yang, *ida* and *pingala*, Shiva and Shakti, right brain and left brain. The longing to find the union of polarities finds expression through ambition, conquest, love, sex, and yoga.

Yoga, as we all know, means union. The simplest form of yoga is to put your hands together in *namaskar*. Namaskar brings harmony between the two polarities within you. Try putting your hands together, bringing both palms together in proper alignment, and looking at someone or something with loving attention. In three to five minutes, you will begin to harmonize.

Namaskar yourself into peace. Namaskar yourself
into love. Namaskar yourself into union. Let us put our
hands together and unite the world. May you unfold your
being with folded hands.

Spirituality and Fast-Forward Karma

When you consciously seek freedom from karma through a spiritual practice, you are essentially on fast-forward. When you
churn up your inner life, certain dimensions of your karma come
to the fore. At such junctures, it is possible to experience intense
pain or discomfort. Of course, this could mean that you have
contracted some ailment. But, frequently, this is just your past
karma surfacing and manifesting itself in one way or another.

The whole point of the spiritual process is to take on more of
a karmic load than your allotted one in order to finish off as
much as possible. It means you do not want to keep repeating
the same cycles again and again. So if you are in an active spiritual process, you may find everything moving at a bewildering
pace. Physical troubles that used to beset you every six months
are now coming up every six hours! This is only because you have
chosen to work out your karma as soon as possible. You are
choosing not to live a sanitized life that regards spirituality as
mere placidity.

If your karma were to unwind slowly, it would probably create small aches over a long period of time. But the fast-forward
of karma often means you might experience intense pain fleet-
ingly. Many people have become less alive and less joyful and
their lives slower and more apathetic because they experience
low-level pain for stretches of time. A spiritual journey simply

cranks up the process so what might have spread over three months or a year happens in a few minutes.

It is important to allow this fast-forward karmic process to happen. Do not suppress it. It is wisest to let your physical body burn up your Allotted Karma as soon as possible. The basis of hatha yoga is just this: You learn to handle pain in the same way as you handle pleasure. If you learn this, you achieve an equanimity that will carry you beyond the turbulence of the karmic process.

In yoga, the practice of kriya often hastens the karmic process without interfering with it. When you put chemicals into the system, however, you are creating another karma for which you pay a price in the future.

Those who are meditative will experience deep levels of joy. But this also opens them up to deep levels of pain. This pain is only for a short duration, however, because their higher level of awareness allows them to work it out more quickly. When you go into deeper levels of meditation, if you take a single wrong step, the effect manifests itself immediately and you will have to correct it. But for the person who lives in relative unawareness, the process may be slow but much deeper. What takes a lifetime could be over on this very day for the spiritually aware person because they immediately take corrective measures.

If you become meditative and still carry negativity, your negative karmas become a thousand times more powerful because you have become that much more sensitive and receptive. Suppose you cultivate the soil and enrich it with manure. The crops will grow well, but the same manure will also enable weeds to grow. Similarly, when you cultivate a meditative state and allow negative emotions to flourish, inner suffering increases dramatically. It is important to be extra cautious about weeding when you are in such a state. Otherwise you will be left with a forest of weeds and no crop!

The reason those on the spiritual path have a daily practice is just this: to ensure that karmic stagnation does not happen. You may already have noticed that if you have a daily practice and you stop it for six months, many recurrent issues—physical, psychological, and social—that have not bothered you for a while start returning. This is how the karmic cycle works. You may have believed you were transformed, but you will suddenly find all kinds of compulsive behaviors returning with a vengeance. Only practice, or sadhana, helps break the cyclical movement of life.

EIGHT

Karma Yoga and the Mental Body

SUTRA #8

*If you experience this moment just once,
you will never be able to fall out of it.*

Plunging into the Present

In the modern world, ruled by the intellect, the mind is far more dominant than ever before. The body is no longer the most powerful presence in our lives. In an age of virtual reality, where lives can be lived out almost entirely in cyberspace, people are sometimes barely aware that they own a body!

However, if we are able to use our mind to make a shift in our perspective, we can make a paradigm shift—one that can create the right ambience for the deeper journey toward liberation.

This is not an invitation to a new philosophy. As a guru, I am not interested in offering spiritual advice. There is nothing new to add to the barrage of spiritual teachings to which we are heir. What I offer is a way, a living process. This is best transmitted during a live program in a controlled atmosphere. But even in a book, a significant shift can occur if the reader is willing and in the right state of openness. What follows is an invitation to a living wisdom. An invitation to shed vast volumes of karmic baggage so we can become receptive to grace.

Now, human beings, as we all know, experience time as three different dimensions: past, present, and future. Our lives and our languages are structured around this.

But let us look at this afresh.

In actual fact, all that you call your past exists only as memory. Do you see this? All the life events that have shaped you; all the work you have ever done; all the money in your bank balance; all the vacations you have been on; all the conversations and arguments you have had; all the relationships of love and hatred and indifference; all the friendships and enmities you have nurtured; all the books you have read and movies you have seen; all the scriptures you have read—all this exists only in your memory.

Similarly, all that you call future exists only as imagination. All that you long for and dread—your dream house; your perfect mate; your baby; your promotion; your pay hike; your beach home; the accolades you believe you deserve; all the horrific illnesses you could contract; all the terrible accidents that could befall all those you love; all the gruesome ways in which you could lose your money, your property, your family, your life; all the apocalyptic ways in which this planet could meet its end— all this exists only in your imagination.

And so these are the *only two things* that you are suffering right now: your memory and your imagination. Nothing more.

Both memory and imagination exist only in your mind. They are aspects of your psychological reality; they have *nothing* to do with the existential reality.

Stop for a moment and ask yourself, When I am not lost in these mental constructs of memory or imagination, where am I?

There can be only one answer to that: the present.

The present is not a creed, a matter of faith. It is a reality. You don't have to *try* to be in the moment. The present isn't an idea. And the fact is, you don't have to try to be in it. You *are* in the moment. *There is nowhere else to be.* Existentially, this is the only truth. It is just that you are not available to it.

Does this mean that you should abandon your memory and imagination?

Certainly not. In any case, we do not wish to destroy karma, because it is the glue that makes our physical and psychological reality possible. However, we do wish to transcend it when we choose. This means seeing one simple fact: your individuality is entirely made up. It is your creation.

Your karma enables you to gather a certain amount of life. What you call "myself" is simply the name you give to the volume of life that you have captured. But if we wipe out all psychological imprints, you as a person will not exist. You will exist as pure life. Existentially, you are life in its essence. In that essential, unmanifest state, you are completely devoid of time and you are completely devoid of karma. You are deathless, indestructible, eternal.

So what is left when the myth of individuality is shattered?

You simply reach the end of cyclical time.

This moment contains an infinite number of possibilities. You can destroy your entire psychological structure and create a new one at this very moment. Or you can stop creating entirely and exist as pure, formless life. This means you have chosen freedom over form, timelessness over temporality, the present moment over cyclical time.

Think about it. Your understanding of time is essentially cyclical. The planet spins once; you call it a day. The moon revolves around the planet; you say it is a month. The planet goes around the sun; you proclaim that it is a year. Everything that is physical is cyclical. In the East, the world of cycles is called samsara. When we talk of transcending karma, we are essentially thinking of how to transcend the cycles of samsara.

Once you break the cycle, there is no "you" and "me" anymore. For individuality exists only in time and space. Once we cross the boundaries of time and space, of memory and imagination, there is no "us" and "them." There is no "here" and "there." There is no "yesterday" and "tomorrow." There is only this moment, and this moment is eternity.

My cell phone has a mind of its own. It organizes my schedules; it anticipates my next word. It is not so different from my body, except that my body is a more sophisticated technology than my phone. I acquired my phone a year ago; I acquired my body over six decades ago. I am separate from both of them. The tragedy is that we have become so identified with our body (and our cell phone!) that we believe life without them is death.

People all over the world look at the entire cosmos on their cell phones. But at the end of the day, all they've been looking at is their phone screens!

Similarly, because you acquired a body and mind, you imagine you are going all over the place. But at the end of your life, you realize that you have just been looking at your projection: the phone screen of your mind. It is like being rudely jolted into reality after a movie, when the lights come on. You haven't moved an inch; you have just been going round and round in exactly the same spot!

The mind can create a cosmos of its own, but everything in it is a projection of your own making. You have begun to believe that each projection is a creation in its own right. It is not.

You have a sense of time and space only because you are looking at everything through the prism of your Accumulated Karma. But if you go beyond your thought, your emotion, and your body and experience this moment just once, you will never be able to fall out of it.

This physical reality that you know is way below one percent of the universe. Even the planet is not forever; it is an inconsequential ball of mud in the larger scheme of things. You are a super-minuscule speck on that. You forget that and pretend that you can create an entire universe based on the little data you have gathered.

You then see yourself as an individual in opposition to the world. You see the larger universe as trying to crush your world. But it is only trying to crush something that doesn't exist! Creation is simply reminding you that you are taking the virtual to be real. It is the magnanimity of creation that allows you an experience of individuality, even though you actually have nothing that you can call your own.

Of course, you can have fun with the game of individuality and the dance of duality. I do not want to discredit your lived experience in any way. But I do want to remind you that it is a game—and one created by you. Go ahead and enjoy the ride, if it appeals to you. Just don't take it too seriously, that's all!

This Moment Is Inevitable

How does all this lead to a paradigm shift?

Here's how.

As we have seen, this moment is all there is. Accepting this is not a formula. It is not a theory. It means seeing reality just the way it is. It means aligning yourself with the way things are, not the way you think they should be.

Once you accept that this moment is all there is, you see that *this moment is inevitable*. It cannot be any other way.

Don't try to make knowledge out of it. Don't philosophize. Don't say, "Yes, all moments are inevitable."

That is not what I am saying. All moments are not inevitable. Only *this* moment is inevitable.

Do you see the difference?

The inevitability of this moment is the only stable speck of time—the fulcrum upon which the entire physical creation rests.

If you are conscious, there is only one place in which you can be.

Now.

Stay with moment-to-moment awareness. Now answer this simple question: Is the next moment inevitable?

No.

If you are consciously in this moment, you will see that only this moment is inevitable.

The next moment?

It is a million possibilities.

If you are aware, you become a positive, dynamic acceptance of this moment. Happiness that one strives for is a natural ambience that you will live in. There is no other way to be, because happiness is not an occasion, a goal, a destination. Happiness is just your constant state of existence. And this is the end of suffering.

This moment is therefore the only doorway both to creation and to the very source of creation. The rest is just hallucination. Your ideas of past and future are entirely delusional. If you consciously accept this moment just the way it is, you arrive at a certain ease within yourself. Ease is a consequence of the relaxation of all you have created. You can, in turn, experience the whole of existence as yourself. Everything becomes a part of you, as creation in its very nature exists as one whole. Knowing this experience is yoga, or the ultimate union.

Most people don't know how to be at ease. Restlessness rules their lives; they are always trying to get somewhere else. But the fact is: *you cannot go anywhere else.*

In your mind, you can go to a million places. You can live in a perennial sense of elsewhereness if you choose. But *the moment you are aware, you are in the present.* Wherever you go, whatever you do, you can be only in this moment. Do what you want, you can be only in this moment. You can think about yesterday; you can think about tomorrow; you can think a million years ahead. But you are still doing it only in this moment.

Does this mean you must never make plans, never reminisce about the past?

Not at all. There is nothing wrong with using the faculties of memory and imagination. They are essential for our survival. We learn from our history and we certainly need to plan for our future. But there is a difference between using the mind and being used by it. It is time to stop being ruled by a hallucination, to stop being tyrannized by a dream.

Now, once you accept something, you own it. Whatever you accept becomes a part of you. Whatever you do not accept stands apart like a huge hurdle.

When I was in university, there was a classmate of mine who joined India's National Cadet Corps. He was told that the paramilitary training would offer him good exercise and good food. After a few months, he was taken to a mock army camp, where he was given sentry duty. This required him to carry a heavy Lee-Enfield 303 rifle while walking up and down near the gate for six hours a day. He was a skinny boy, and he simply could not carry the rifle. He felt like his arm was coming loose.

He complained to his commandant. "Sir, I cannot carry this rifle. It is too heavy for me. Give me some other responsibility. I cannot do this sentry duty."

The commandant simply stared at him.

The boy scaled down. "Or let me use a stick instead of this rifle," the boy pleaded. "The rifle is too heavy—and it doesn't even have a trigger! In any case, no enemy is really going to attack. Let me use a stick instead."

The commandant said nothing.

"Sir, please," the boy implored him.

The commandant reached out and caught hold of him by his shirt. "You see this? This is a uniform. Once you are in this uniform, you are a soldier. Why are you *carrying* a rifle? It is a part of you."

This statement had a profound impact on the boy. After six hours, even the strongest boys in the camp wanted to throw down their rifles. But this boy suddenly had no problem. He simply couldn't put it down. It had become a part of him!

Whenever pain enters your life, you tend to wonder, Why me? Even my mother-in-law didn't get it! Of all the people in the world, why *me*?

But once you accept something, it becomes a part of you. Even for a moment, if you accept something as a part of you, you attain a profound sense of harmony. You are attuned to life. If your acceptance is total, you can experience the whole of existence as part of yourself.

Can existence really become a part of you?

Now, that seems logically impossible. It *is* logically impossible, but that is the truth.

As you are a part of existence, existence is also a part of you.

As a drop is part of the ocean, the ocean is also part of the drop. This is because time and space are not absolutes; they can be stretched and contracted as well. Yoga has always said you can pack the whole of creation into a mustard seed! Modern physics confirms that time and space are not what we once thought they were. So once you transcend the limitations of your logic, you also transcend the limitations of time and space. If you become absolute acceptance, then everything—past, present, future—is *here and now*.

Is this some kind of magic?

No, this is reality, the most spectacular magic of creation.

Accepting this moment is not a formula or a concept. It is the very basis of creation. It is in the lap of this moment that creation is happening. All you need to do is to accept this moment in its entirety. An uninhibited response to it, with all that you are—in thought, emotion, and the very life that you are—delivers you to a blessed reality—the very source of creation.

Once you have come to this planet as a human being, if you do not experience your universality—the incredible possibility implicit in this moment—your human form has gone to waste. To merely eat, sleep, reproduce, and die, you do not need the sophisticated body, mind, and awareness you have been gifted with. If this tremendous gift is not explored, it is a terrible shame.

The Complexity of Conditioning

What prevents human beings from discovering the profoundly transformative potential of the present moment?

The answer is simple: a vagrant mind.

The human mind is an infinitely complex mechanism. If you seek to liberate yourself from karma, it is important to have some understanding of how this elaborate mechanism functions.

This highly intricate machinery is necessary for our physical survival. It can, however, often become a barrier to our longing for freedom.

As we have seen, you may endlessly discuss freedom, but there is no such thing as freedom when the very way you think, feel, and perceive life is conditioned by your past experience. From the day you were born, your parents, your family, your culture, your religion, your education, your social context have worked upon you, determining who you are right now. So your mind is very deeply conditioned by your past.

This conditioning is what we call karma. Your entire volume of past action, performed knowingly or unknowingly, has shaped who you are today. This has such a viselike grip on you that there is no question of free will. The very way you see the world is determined by your karmic lens. Let us look at the mental mechanism that creates your karma.

Gautama the Buddha, a great scientist of the human mind, speaks of four aspects of the mind: *vinyana* (cognition), *sanya* (recognition), *vedana* (sensation), and *sankara* (reaction).

Now, let us suppose a sound comes to your ears. It enters the first aspect of your mind. Vinyana cognizes that this is a sound, not a smell, taste, or sight. Sanya recognizes the sound: that this is a person speaking, a bird chirping, an automobile engine starting up, and so on. How does it recognize it? Every sound you have ever heard has been recorded, so a vast library of sounds exists within you. Without a past impression, there is no possibility of recognition. If, for instance, you hear the sound of a woodpecker for the very first time, your mind will be confused. But ten days later, if you hear it again, sanya will recognize it immediately.

If there are some young people next door playing heavy-metal music, you may go into ecstasy, but your grandfather may have a nervous breakdown! The same sound creates a pleasant sensation in one person and drives the other crazy. Now, if you recognize the sound, vedana swings into action and produces a sensation. If you recognize this as music, pleasant sensations will happen; if you recognize this as noise, unpleasant sensations will happen. It is not the sound itself, but the way it is imprinted on you that makes you recognize it as pleasant or unpleasant. So the very way in which you experience life—whether you see it as sweet or sour, beautiful or ugly, pleasant or unpleasant—is *your responsibility*, as your ability to respond is what determines the nature of your experience.

You are a sensory being. Your entire experience of life is a certain sensation. If you don't feel a certain sensation, you are not even aware that that part of your body exists. When your leg goes numb for a few moments, you are not even sure if it exists. It is vedana that reminds you that you exist by giving you the experience of sensation. The way you recognize the sensory input is the way you experience life. Vinyana, sanya, and vedana—cognition, recognition, and sensation—are automatic and take place in a split second.

However, the fourth part of the mind is related to reaction and is entirely in your conscious control. If a pleasant sensation arises and you say you love it, your sankara immediately says "Oh, he loves it. Store it in the love bag." Now it is stored in your love bag forever. If an unpleasant sensation arises, and you strongly feel "I hate it," sankara immediately says "He hates it. Store it in the hate bag." It is then stored in the hate bag forever. If you find yourself oscillating between craving and aversion, love and hate, your karma is growing at a rapid pace; your bondage is intensifying. If you have strong likes and dislikes, your suffering is also more intense.

But another scenario is also possible. If a sensation arises, you have a choice whether to react. Once you are able to exercise this choice, you simply experience the sensation for what it is. If you generate a strong reaction, you will distort the experience. But if you remain equanimous, the karma attached to that type of sensation begins to crumble within you.

With equanimity, your entire structure of karma begins to collapse. All it takes is a willingness to experience everything the way it is. You are not avoiding experience or pursuing it. You are simply open to enjoying the different flavors of life without seeking one and escaping the other.

Isn't that the whole point of your sojourn on this planet: to experience as much of life as possible before you fall dead?

So begin with this profound realization: *this moment is inevitable*.

Put differently, one might say, allow this simple truth to percolate into you: *my ability to respond is boundless*.

If you are aware of this truth, you will see that so much that seems to be restricting you right now will vanish in just twenty-four hours! Being in awareness for just three minutes will enable you to see an immediate difference. Once you are able to steadily maintain this awareness, you will find a time comes when there is no difference between you and a Buddha.

As your acceptance deepens, you also move into higher and higher levels of freedom. Acceptance is freedom from the blame game, freedom from the drama of "othering," freedom from the dance of duality. There is only you in this moment and no one else. Who then can you possibly blame?

But when you keep resisting, you are creating deeper levels of bondage. Seeing that your ability to respond is limitless is profoundly important, because this ability goes way beyond your present level of understanding and perception.

Now, the moment people hear that they have the ability to respond even to events that happened before they were born, they are given to dismissing this as nonsense: "I am responsible for things that happened before my birth? This is outrageous! This is crossing the limits of logic!"

But let us look at it another way.

Suppose my grandfather had given twenty-five million dollars to your grandfather as a loan. Today, I read my grandfather's old diary and see that he has clearly made note of this transaction on a particular day. My grandfather passed away three days after this loan was made, and so the money was never repaid.

I have proof of the transaction. So I come to you and say "My grandfather lent your grandfather this sum of money before we or our fathers were born. I have proof. Since we are friends, I will waive the interest. But please return the principal amount."

What would you say to that?

Obviously, you would say "Sheer nonsense! Why am I responsible for something that happened before I was born? Go ask my grandfather for it!"

But let us say the tables are reversed. I am enjoying my property, but you found some old papers this morning that clearly say that this property belongs to your grandfather. What would you do? How would you act? You would immediately have contacted your lawyers, wouldn't you?

If your grandfather made wealth or owned property before you were born, you would definitely take responsibility for it. But if he had taken a loan, of course you are not responsible!

This is an ancient social game: heads, I win; tails, you lose.

The fact is, your responsibility—whether you like it or not, know it or not—goes way beyond your present levels of understanding. If you accept this fact, your life naturally comes to a certain ease and harmony. The more you start seeing that you are responsible for your life, the closer you move toward your liberation. If you try to pass the buck to somebody, you will start moving toward your entanglement.

Let us say you were walking on a street and some passerby stepped on your foot and broke it. You are in great pain, and you hold the passerby responsible. When you hold someone responsible for your pain, you tend to wish the same to them. On the other hand, if you were able to think "What happened is unfortunate, but if my leg is broken, it is my karma," you would take responsible action, rather than fritter away time and energy complaining, cursing your fate, or planning your vendetta.

Which is a more intelligent way to exist?

Don't make the mistake of thinking karma is fatalism. Acknowledging karma means that you see that your life is one hundred percent your doing. If you see this, you will create your life the way you want it, rather than sitting around feeling helpless, cursing your parents' genes or your current circumstances. Seeing your life as self-created, rather than as an accidental phenomenon—this is the basis of karma. This is an empowered life that will naturally move toward liberation.

SADHANA

Most human beings do not realize the tremendous power of creativity they have been endowed with. This is because most of their creations are determined by their compulsiveness, not by their freedom. Anything created by limitation will be limited. But if you see your ability to respond as limitless, the power to create is super-enhanced.

Here is something you can try for yourself. If you drop your self-image completely, you will find yourself in a state of great freedom. You now have the power to live without a self-image at all. You also have the power to transform your image altogether. Basically, you can pick up an image and drop it at will. Either way, nothing will stick to you.

I will not tell you how you should be. But stop now and create yourself anew in your mind. Start with the skeletal structure. Slowly, move into the flesh and blood.

Close your eyes and visualize how you would like other people to experience you. How would you like the fundamental nature of your thought and emotion to be? What kind of impact would you like to have on the world?

Create a whole new being.

Then see if this new image is any closer to your notion of the divine than the old. Is it really better than the earlier image? Examine it in great detail. Is this new image more capable, more human, more loving, more blissful?

Visualize this new image as powerfully as you can. Make it come alive within you. If your thought is powerful enough, if your visualization is powerful enough, it can even break through the bonds of karma.

Here is an opportunity to transcend all your limitations of thought, emotion, and action. Here is an opportunity to consciously craft yourself to become the creation you want to be.

Creating Distance from the Karmic Structure

The primary aim of meditation is to create a certain distance between you and your physical, mental, and energy bodies. Your mental body is a major manufacturing unit of karma. If you see that your mind is the principal source of karma, you are on the right path. Once there is a distance between you and the mind, there is a distance from the past. Now all those memories are available when you need them, but they no longer have the power to rule you.

The aim is one day to create a situation within you in which you have the living experience *I am not the accumulations of my mind.* Now your karma has no power over you. This is the first step toward freedom.

There is a growing trend of attempting past-life regressions in the hope of looking into one's karmic structure. This is absolutely unnecessary if one is on a spiritual path. Sifting through the content of your mind is an endless and pointless exercise. The spiritual seeker does not want to drop karma selectively. The aim is to drop the package entirely.

Once there is a clear space between you and your mind, your karma empties very rapidly. You have now stopped creating new stock, which helps enormously. The old stock will flow out very quickly with the passage of time.

You are now able to see *My mind belongs to me, but I am not my mind.* It is like driving a car. The engine responds to everything you intend it to do, but it is not you. When you get deeply involved with your car, you may see it as an extension of yourself. Many people do! But when you are able to distance yourself from your mind, your capacity to make it do what you want it to do increases. Once you can separate yourself this way, you do not have to worry about karma ever again.

The basis of karma is simple: you are the source of all your baggage. When you clearly perceive this, your essential quality changes. If you see someone else as the source, you will always be distracted, disoriented, bitter, frustrated, agitated, and angry. When you see yourself as the source, you are centered. Your energies are now focused within you. You are no longer enacting rituals of blame and rage in your head. You are no longer enslaved to your external environment or to your mind.

Once you understand karma as your responsibility, you are free. Once you distance yourself from your mind, you are also free. Both approaches work.

Reclaiming Responsibility

It happened.

On a certain day, Shankaran Pillai went to the bar. He settled down at the bar counter. "See, I need a drink, but I don't have any money on me right now," he told the bartender.

"Please leave," said the bartender immediately. "We don't entertain such people here."

Shankaran Pillai was unfazed. "Wait a moment. I can show you something. If you're impressed by it, you give me a free drink. If you aren't, I promise to go away without a word."

Then Shankaran Pillai proceeded to pull out a toad from his pocket. He placed it on the counter.

The bartender asked, bored, "Are you going to tell me that if I kiss it, it will turn into a princess?"

"No, no," Shankaran Pillai assured him. "Just wait." And he pulled out a hamster from another pocket. "This hamster," he announced, "can recite chapters from the Bible for you."

"Hah!" the bartender scoffed. "Don't bullshit me, man."

"Just listen," Shankaran Pillai said.

And the hamster promptly recited Galatians 5.

"Hey, this is incredible!" the bartender exclaimed and fixed Shankaran Pillai a drink.

Shankaran Pillai accepted the drink and put the hamster back in his pocket. "You know, I'm never done with one drink," he said. "I can make this toad recite the Bible, too. Ask for any chapter."

"How about Genesis 3?" asked the impressed bartender. The toad promptly reeled it off.

The bartender was amazed. He offered Shankaran Pillai yet another drink.

Shankaran Pillai downed it and announced, "And now this toad is for sale."

Everyone in the bar immediately started bidding. The bidding was fast and furious. The toad was finally sold for two hundred dollars.

As Shankaran Pillai was about to give the toad to the highest bidder, the bartender held him by the collar and pulled him across the counter. "You idiot!" he hissed. "You're giving away a talking toad for two hundred dollars! I can get you two million if you're willing to split."

Shankaran Pillai said calmly, "No, no, it doesn't matter. What they're paying is enough."

He collected his two hundred dollars and handed over the toad. The excited man who bought it ran out of the bar to show off his new acquisition.

The bartender told Shankaran Pillai, "You're a nutcase. A talking toad for just two hundred dollars!"

Shankaran Pillai said, "Don't worry. It's just that my hamster is a ventriloquist."

This absurd state of affairs is actually the way many people lead their lives. They choose to outsource the responsibility all the time—to their equivalent of the hamster.

Most of the time, people pass the buck to their old karma. The tragedy is that in the process, they miss the enormous potential of this moment. They barter away the transformative power of the present by ensuring the future is a repetition of their past.

Your old karma is not the problem. The problem is that your present karma is looking for an escape route. It wants to blame someone else. It wants to go to the past, or the future, and escape the present. And so the same old cycle of victimhood and passivity perpetuates itself. Stop and see: you might well find you are doing it right *now*.

Yes, it is true that your old karma creates certain tendencies that influence you. However, every human being has awareness enough to overcome these tendencies. Not a single person needs to be enslaved by their hereditary blueprint. Each of us has a choice: the choice to transcend our karmic inheritance or to be tyrannized by it.

How many times do you overhear people say something along the lines of the ventriloquist hamster? "I really want to control my temper, but you know how it is: my father's genes . . ." Or "I wish I could start cleaning up my street, but I live in such an apathetic neighborhood." With every statement of this kind, you are not merely making sweeping verdicts about your past; *you are writing off your future before you live it.*

Irrespective of past karma, if you handle your present moment right, things can change fundamentally. This is the beauty of being human. It doesn't matter what kind of baggage you are carrying; if you are willing to be absolutely conscious, the past has no impact upon you. I have seen this in countless numbers of people. With just a little better understanding of the mechanics of their mind, even without any serious sadhana, they find themselves more joyful than ever before. Without knowing why, they find themselves walking with a new spring in their step, singing in the shower, or whistling during the day. In the Inner

Engineering program I conduct, even before we initiate people into an energy action called a kriya, just hearing about the workings of the mind frees them up in many ways.

What you call karma—the bags of tendencies and predispositions you carry with you—is only in your memory and imagination. So if you inhabit this moment deeply, fully, completely, you have dropped your karmic load.

It is time to let go of the past. Live consciously, and you will see that this moment cannot be fragmented into past and future, into now and then. All that ever was in this creation is only in this moment, and all that will ever be is only in this moment.

The present is your only address. The here and now is your only abode.

NINE

Karma Yoga and the Energy Body

SUTRA #9

It is not about performing miracles.
It is about recognizing the miracle of life that you are.

Fixing the Destination

I often say that there is only one thing I am really good at: making places and people crackle with energy. Everything else that I do—all my travels around the world, giving talks, conducting programs, initiating environmental, educational, and cultural projects—is incidental. This does not mean I do not value the work that I do. I throw myself wholeheartedly into all of it. But my primary area of expertise is life energy. I am an energy mechanic above all else.

Karma yoga on the level of the energy, or pranic, body is vital for many reasons. For one, it can transform or regenerate the energy body in such a way that it is not just born anew but actually stays new. No matter how much exercise or hatha yoga you do, how carefully you watch your diet, your physical body will age and decay. The mental body is a wonderful instrument, but it can also rust with age. There are many who find that their memory is not as sharp as when they were younger. The energy body, however, can be completely unaffected by the aging process. You can maintain it just the way it was when you were born and keep it in mint-fresh condition until you die. The impact of a strong energy body on your life and on the world around you is tremendous. For many, it can seem near-miraculous.

At the Isha programs, participants are initiated into what is known as a kriya—a powerful yogic process that renews and re-invigorates the energy body. I call it the path of inner action, because it does not involve the physical or mental body. It is action purely on the level of energy. If practiced regularly, it ensures that the energy body stays vibrant and alive. If you are able to maintain your energy body like that of a newborn infant every moment of your life, you will find that external and internal circumstances invariably unfold in the best possible way for you.

There is yet another reason why working with the energy body is beneficial. It is the most direct way of addressing the tricky dimension of one's karmic inheritance. I call it tricky because the karmic residue is not a body by itself, but a dimension that occupies the physical, mental, and energy bodies. Addressing karma on the physical level is important, as we have seen: it can cleanse the elements; help minimize physical memory; and through the practice of hatha yoga, it can revitalize and upgrade the system. Addressing karma on the mental level is also important: it can create a paradigm shift in the way you live your life and inhabit this moment. However, when you address your karma on the level of energy, the process is deeper and swifter, and it rapidly accelerates change on all the other levels.

Above all, it is capable of changing your destination. Yoga on the level of the physical body can bring well-being; on the level of the mental body, it can bring joy, equanimity, and peace; but on the level of the energetic, it ensures that you are heading only toward your liberation.

If you do physical work, the physical body is exercised and will grow well. If you do mental work, your mental body is exercised and will grow considerably. Most people, unfortunately, never exercise their energy body, so it remains weak. This is why so many people in the world who have money, wealth, fame, even a social media following, still feel insignificant. A yogi has no such feeling because their energy body is highly developed.

The same life event could leave a different imprint on different people. A marriage breaking up could be a boon for one person. But another may be mentally broken, another physically sick. Whatever you eat, drink, and breathe is energy. Whether you transform it into physical, mental, or life energy is up to you. Energy is neither created nor destroyed; it is only transformed.

It happened.

Shankaran Pillai was looking for a new residence. While apartment hunting, he met a landowner. The landowner asked him, "Where have you been staying all these years?"

Shankaran Pillai mentioned that he had been in one part of town a month ago, another part of town two months ago, and in a completely different district six months ago.

The landowner grew suspicious. "Why do you keep shifting residence? Do you have many enemies?"

"No, no, I don't have a single enemy," Shankaran Pillai declared breezily. "But for some reason, all my friends hate me."

Describing enemies as friends is, of course, mere euphemistic wordplay! It bears no relationship to reality. Many choose to live their lives at this superficial level. They opt for self-improvement rather than self-transformation, hoping that a life of tepid affability and general agreeability will take them to the ultimate. They forget that the social has nothing to do with the existential.

This is why karma yoga has to be approached on many levels. Merely working on the levels of the physical and the psychological is not enough. If you clean your mental slate of karmic substance, you may be appreciated socially because there is a certain peace, joy, and sweetness about your presence. People may enjoy being around you because you've cleaned up your mind. But this still does not change the direction in which you are going. You will still be influenced by the residual impact of lifetimes of experience that lead you by your tendencies. Only if you begin to clean the energy body of karmic content will you begin to move in a new direction. Instead of being ruled by tendencies, you now begin to become a conscious being.

The kriya Shambhavi Mahamudra that I initiate people into during my Inner Engineering programs is significant for this reason. It picks off the karmic material from the energy system and thereby changes your destination. It would be possible to devote the program to turning out pleasant human beings. This would meet with great social approval. But whether you are pleasant or unpleasant has no spiritual relevance. Once you transform the content of the energy body, the fundamentals of life will begin to alter. You are now hugely empowered to begin your march toward freedom.

The Yoga of Heat and Light

I am often asked by people how they can burn their karma. I tell them that burning karma is relevant only up to a certain point. It gives you the necessary clarity to look at life in an unclouded way and offers you a certain freedom from compulsions, anxieties, and fears. But if you burn up your entire karmic stock, the physical and mental bodies will not be able to sustain themselves. For this reason, retaining the body is a perennial challenge for an enlightened being.

For most spiritual practitioners, after some amount of karmic burning, it is best to perform a kind of sadhana that gives you a certain distance from the karma. The presence of karma will keep your practice going; at the same time, the practice gives you a certain gap between you and your body and mind. This is the kind of person that is urgently needed on this planet today. Most of what needs to be done in this world does not get accomplished because people have no capacity to distance themselves from their karmic compulsions.

Once you have a certain distance from the karma, it doesn't matter what kind of karma you have. Your karma adds color to the world, in fact. The world is full of all kinds of crazy, unique human beings, and that is wonderful as long as they are not compulsive! If there are no compulsions, there is no good or bad, correct or incorrect way to be. Everything is part of the great, colorful tapestry of life.

Do not forget: Compulsions can be of many kinds. Whether you smoke or drink or pray all day, your actions can still be compulsive. Whatever you do, if it is done with joy and gratitude and if it moves you toward freedom from cycles, it makes all the difference. If a certain prayerful attitude grows within you out of your joy and gratitude, that is beautiful. It is the context, not the content of your life, that determines karmic accumulation.

This is why the eight limbs of yoga (ashtanga yoga, as it is known) are structured in a particular way: the first three limbs (yama, niyama, and asana) are considered to be the fire aspect and are purificatory; the last four (pratyahara, dharana, dhyana, and samadhi) are considered to be the light aspect and are enlightening. The fourth limb—pranayama—is considered to be the intermediate transitory step, combining both fire and light.

Yama and *niyama* are simple guidelines, the dos and don'ts on the spiritual path, such as nonviolence; commitment to truth; not stealing; not hoarding wealth; purity; cleanliness; practice; and so on. They create the right atmosphere for one's spiritual evolution. Once a person is enlightened, these dos and don'ts are of little relevance. When compassion within you is overflowing and divinity has come to the fore, no rules need to be prescribed. Human nature at this point knows exactly what needs to be done in a given situation. But these simple moral strictures were identified for the benefit of those starting out on the path.

Asanas are, of course, the many physical yoga postures practiced by the seeker in a certain state of awareness. They are a way of manipulating your inner energies in a particular direction, a way of kneading the body toward a higher possibility. If you have ever made bread, you will know that the quality of the bread depends on how efficiently the dough has been kneaded. The quality of an earthen pot depends on how well the clay has been kneaded. Similarly, asanas are about elevating consciousness by thoroughly kneading the body. This is how deep the science of yoga is: it journeys from the outer to the inner, reminding us that working consciously on the physical level can alter the way one thinks, feels, and experiences life and can ultimately lead one to higher spiritual possibilities.

The fourth limb, *pranayama*, entails consciously working with prana, or life energy. It is the intermediate stage of both fire and light, because it is both purgative and enlightening in nature.

Pratyahara—turning inward—is a particularly important limb of yoga and is most challenging in modern times, when the world is more distracted by external stimulation than ever before. It entails looking at even the physical and the psychological as external accumulations and spells a complete withdrawal from body and mind.

Dharana is constant unbroken attention toward the inner, based on the premise that whatever you pay unwavering attention to is what you become connected with. In an age dominated by electronic media and a virtual epidemic of people diagnosed with ADHD, this limb, too, is more challenging than ever before.

Dhyana is a state of immersion, or meditation, when there is no longer a divide between you and the inner world (to which you have paid attention during dharana). Two have now become one.

In the final stage, *samadhi*, one has dissolved into nothing. There is absolute equanimity because the discriminatory mind has subsided. The beyond now makes its presence felt.

Purification, or karmic burning, is necessary for those who are entangled and compulsive. Without that burning, most people will not be able to meditate. But once meditation begins, the path is no longer about burning; it is instead an illuminating process of creating a certain distance between yourself and your physical and mental dimensions. This is the journey to freedom.

Most spiritual practitioners will vouch for this. Ninety percent cannot meditate; only after a practice that fires them and burns up compulsive karmas can they close their eyes and sit still. So the ideal sadhana is a balance between the fire and the light aspects. Personally, I am fine with the fire aspect, because I cannot stand insipidity. I prefer rage to tameness and lifelessness! But those who are on fire all the time do not fit into social situations easily. So it is best to create a balance between the two.

Once your Allotted Karma (prarabdha) is handled, a certain inner space is freed up within you. This gives you the room to perceive life with a certain clarity. You need not work out everything else, because you now see that the entire karmic influence is illusory. Once you have that clarity of realization, it is easy to drop it when necessary.

Working out your entire Accumulated Karma (sanchita) is a very long process, because the accumulation is massive. So do not try to investigate the content of your warehouse; it will take forever to go through, and it might well engulf you! The danger of sifting through your karma is that you could well find precious elements that you want to preserve. Just handle the Allotted Karma and make use of the clear space to drop the Accumulated Karma altogether. The moment you close the retail outlet, the warehouse looks like meaningless trash! So when the time comes, you simply dispose of the entire warehouse wholesale—with all its content and storage facility.

It is the sun that has turned water into a cloud and given it a silver lining. But the cloud is now blocking the sun! You could write endless poetry about this exquisite silver-laced cloud, but you will end up missing the sun. This is the nature of karma. As beautiful as it may look, it blocks the source of creation. There may be beauty in some aspects of karma. But do not forget the source from which it has sprung. The source may be no-thing, but implicit in it is a great possibility: *the possibility to become everything*.

SADHANA

While every kriya requires an initiation, there is one kriya that I offer that requires no initiation. This is the Isha Kriya, a simple daily practice that enhances health, dynamism, material and spiritual well-being; offers a means to cope with the hectic pace of modern life; and empowers one to live life to its fullest potential. It is a reminder that there is much more to us than our body and our mind. Those who are interested in exploring this three-stage practice will find it on the Sadhguru app (isha.sadhguru.org/app).

Karma and the Alignment of Bodies

I am often asked what my message is as a guru.

It amuses me, because I have none. I tell people: You are not studying with me. I have nothing to teach. I want you to get lost! I want to invite you to that place of borderless ignorance—that the ancients have called enlightenment—and the only way to get there is to lose yourself. There is no other way.

Teachings will not get you through the many insidious karmic blocks in your life. The karmic walls are like sheets of glass. If they were like walls of brick, you could see them and you could break them. But the problem with sheets of glass is that everything seems to be open, but when you try to reach out, you are locked in.

A teaching, after a certain period of time, becomes a block by itself. You will twist it to your convenience. People have done this to teachings all over the world. Initially, a teaching has an impact on you because it is new and you have no clue as to how it works. But over a period of time, you will start twisting it to your convenience. You will make the teaching support you. This is counterproductive, because the teaching is not meant to support you; it is meant to demolish you!

Once a teaching has become a source of convenience, it is no good. This is why a guru talks from so many different dimensions that seem contrary. The aim is not to allow you to settle anywhere. The moment you settle, you will start using the teaching to your advantage.

This is also why a guru always offers an energy-based practice. Just doing a daily kriya—every morning, sitting and breathing in a certain way—can decimate these karmic blocks. If you don't fully understand the teachings, it's okay. If you keep doing the practice, after some time, you find a new sense of openness and freedom in you. That is always the bedrock you can rely on.

Work on the level of the energy body is about an entire recycling of your energy. When this recycling is under way, it will bring back many impulses, compulsive behavioral patterns, mental habits, and emotional whirlpools. This is inevitable, and it is nothing to be afraid of. This is simply what we mean by karma. When you start cultivating your energy to access a different dimension, the karmic cleansing is inevitable.

This is because the whole karmic structure is being dismantled on some level. With constant practice, the aspiration is to unburn the pot, to dissolve it into pure clay. You are melting the frozen complex of habits and predispositions into pure energy. Only when your energies become this fluid can you sit and meditate. This is because you have now become pure life: you are no longer a bundle of thoughts and impressions. You are in a state of receptivity to grace.

Remember this: there is no utility to a spiritual process. You cannot use it, but you can be transformed by it. Transformation means that you lose your original form and are completely willing to take on new forms. You become an unburnt pot, as it were. You can no longer be filled with water, but, as pure clay, you are capable of taking on an endless number of forms.

There is a well-known Indian folktale about the immortal love of Sohni and Mahiwal. Sohni crosses the river each night to meet her forbidden lover, Mahiwal. Since she belongs to a family of potters, she uses an earthen pot to stay afloat and make her way across the river. But one night, her sister-in-law, who wants to sabotage her secret romance, substitutes an unburnt pot for a burnt one. Inevitably, the pot melts, and Sohni is engulfed by the swirling waters—a tragic end to this love story.

Try as we might, neither love nor the spiritual process can ever be made utilitarian. They are simply part of the beauty of life. The moment you try to harness love or spirituality, you find your arms are empty. The moment you try to concretize them, you end up with a marriage or a religion. You may acquire many other things—a home, a family, a god, a heaven—but you lose the very exuberance of life. When you try to institutionalize an inner experience, all you are left with is an institution!

So once your energies begin to rise, you will find your life suddenly seems more eventful than before, internally and externally. The important thing is not to hesitate, but to keep the practice going full throttle. The yogic kriyas are structured in such a way that they will never cause you any harm.

As we have seen earlier, there can sometimes be a mismatch between the physical body and the energy body. Suppose you took a little car and attached a powerful engine to it—it could be a disaster. The car would fall apart, not because the engine is bad, but because it is too good. Similarly, if your energy body is greatly enhanced without enhancing the physical body or work-ing with the karmic substance, it is possible that one or the other will collapse.

Any attempt to empower the energy body, therefore, must be accompanied by work on every other level. Before people are initiated into powerful kriyas, they need to do a rigorous amount of sadhana. Without physical practice, people cannot experience the kriyas in all their depth and intensity.

When preparing for initiation into powerful kriyas, prac-titioners must also prepare the mind. They need to expand their set of identifications, to widen their understanding of who they are. When they are reminded that their ability to respond extends to the entire cosmos (not just to a family and community); that inclusive involvement is far less entangling than selective involvement; that they are parents not just to their children but to the entire world, the karmic structure loosens considerably. Now it can accommodate a considerable expansion of the energy body.

If energies expand when the karmic substance sits tight upon you, you could feel like you are being ripped apart. This can be hugely disruptive to your life. If you are not able to endure it, an enhancement of the energy body is pointless. It is ideal, there-fore, to expand the karmic structure in such a way that it is able to withstand the intensity that arises in the energy body during kriya yoga.

When My Energies Touched the Peak

The ways in which energy transformation can manifest physi-cally is something I know firsthand. At the age of twenty-five, when I had my first experience of life beyond my physical and mental faculties on a hill in the city of Mysore, I had no idea what had hit me.

Things started changing rapidly after that. Much was internal, but there were external changes, too, that no one could miss. My voice changed, for one. The timbre and quality were distinctly different. The quality of my gaze, even the shape of my eyes, seemed to change, and my gait was dramatically altered. I tried to resume my old way of walking, but I could not. The very shape of my body had changed. And I am in absolutely no doubt that the shape of my brain changed as well!

The realignment of the chakras—or energy centers—in the human system can produce dramatic results. Energy interventions can completely rewire the system and alter the impact of genetic, evolutionary, and elemental memory. It is these dimensions of memory that unconsciously restrict us in many ways. To become free from their impact or to learn to disconnect from them when necessary is a very important aspect of yogic practice.

SADHANA

Depending on the volume or type of karma you have gathered, you have developed certain vasanas that make you move in certain directions and attract certain life situations and people toward you.

If you find that you are constantly attracting the wrong people into your life or drawing unpleasant situations toward you, it is important to pause, take a backward step, and see how to re-draw this software that has been unconsciously written into yourself.

It is like this: Suppose you are driving and your car

goes out of control. What is the first thing you would do? You might want to gift it to your enemy, perhaps! But after that tempting thought, the first thing to do is to apply the brakes and stop it, isn't it? It is the same with your life. When things are going out of control for no explainable reason, you need to turn off the engine for a while.

Bring the whole machinery of thought, emotion, and action to a halt for a short while. Just the act of pausing and attending to your interiority for a short period will make the difference. You will see; things will correct themselves.

You need to do nothing else. You do not need to call for divine intervention. You need not call for angelic help or astral guidance. You simply need to pause. You will find that your mind and body work miraculously after this, simply because you gave your system the necessary time to fix and re-draw itself the way it wants.

Sacred Spaces and the Karmic Fast-Forward

Energy interventions are possible in many ways. One is through kriya yoga under the guidance of a master; another is by simply living in a space that is energetically vibrant and consecrated in a particular way.

There are many empowered sacred sites in the world. These energy centers—called *teertha* in Sanskrit—are simply an invitation to seekers to sit and marinate. Like soaking a soiled cloth in detergent, merely soaking in the energy of these places can remove karmic stains that you are unaware of.

The powerful spiritual legacy of countless mystics pervades the Velliangiri Mountains in southern India. The Isha Yoga

Center in Coimbatore is situated at the foothills of these majestic mountains, a location offering tremendous possibilities for spiritual growth. The center itself has been consecrated in a powerful way so as to accelerate the karmic process.

Making use of such a place does not take any belief. People don't have to see me as their guru to make use of it. It is even absolutely fine if people have a problem with me! If they know how to make use of the space, everything they could possibly need for their spiritual growth is right here. I encourage people everywhere to come experience this possibility. The place is simply loaded with energy. It is the kind of place where transformations that people would consider miraculous are possible. All it takes is to simply close your eyes, sit in the space, and soak it in.

As a guru, I am often asked why I don't perform miracles. I point out that we are surrounded by miracles all the time. The soil that you walk upon transforms itself into flower and fruit, a flower transforms filth into fragrance, time transforms a rock into a diamond. The miracle that I am, the miracle that I want to manifest on this planet, is that it is possible to be involved and immersed and engaged in this world and yet remain untouched by it. There are many around me today who embody this miracle. This, for me, is the only miracle that counts.

There are sites all over the world where immense spiritual power is centered around a specific form or sanctum. The Isha Center has the Dhyanalinga and the Linga Bhairavi, which are powerful energy centers.

However, what is more unusual in the center is that the entire space is saturated with spiritual energy. This is, for one, because there are multiple consecrated shrines across the entire premises. This is also because of those wonderful mystics who have lived in these surrounding mountains; it is their aspiration and intention to make this grace available to all. It has been a privilege for me to create a center in a land sanctified by their presence.

Different energetically intense spaces offer different possibilities. But at the Isha Yoga Center, we ensure that the only possibility is to fast-forward karma and hasten the spiritual process. Nothing else is relevant. There are many places all over the world that pulsate with raw energy, but this is one where the energy is calibrated to assist you on every step of the spiritual path.

Once the energy of a place is set in a certain direction with a particular intensity, nothing will escape its influence. Every being in the vicinity will start moving toward it, unconsciously or consciously. This has nothing to do with a teaching. It is just life longing for itself.

Certain geographies can certainly accelerate the karmic process. But do not expect it to be joyful all the time. In intense spin cycles, there can be moments that are challenging. But it is all worth it when you find yourself emerging from the cyclical nature of the karmic process and from the terrible rut of rehashing the same story over and over.

The longing for liberation, or *mukti*, is not because life is miserable. When you are miserable, you long for heaven, not liberation. The longing for liberation arises only when life is good, but you naturally want to evolve to the next dimension. You do not want to go through the tedium of the same cycles time and again.

Karma and the Energy Body at Birth

One can know many things about a child at birth. Most people notice that some infants are bright-eyed and observant; others seem quieter; some move their limbs more; others are less active.

Traditionally, in India, within the first eleven days of their child's birth, parents often took the infant to a yogi or seer for a blessing. This is because the karmic substance is still fluid at this stage. Before the baby's personality begins to get consolidated, they want a blessing that can ensure that the child's life journey will be a smooth and seamless one.

The actual karmic journey begins even before that. Somewhere between forty and forty-eight days after conception, the karmic fiber begins to tighten. It is like a spring coil. Depending on past information, the strength of the physical body, the nature of the parent, the type of conception, and various other factors, the karmic fiber chooses a certain amount of information that winds itself into a coiled spring.

If I look at the tension of the karmic fiber, I can often estimate when a person was born and approximately when they are going to die. Of course, accidents or unintended damage to the body can occur, so not every person is able to work out their Allotted Karma. However, barring accidents, most people's karmic coil unwinds at a certain pace.

Those who are capable of sitting still will find that their karma unwinds rapidly. Those who lead active lives pile up new karma, so the process is slower. Nonetheless, the karmic coil continues to unwind. So it is possible to assess how long the karmic journey will continue for a person if they live a standard life. If they come in touch with a guru, of course, these predictions are no longer possible. With a spiritual master's intervention, the karma can be released rapidly, if necessary.

Aging and Death

Toward the end of a person's life, as the Allotted Karma reaches completion, the energy body begins to grow feeble. As a result, the physical body grows increasingly feeble as well, and the capacity of the energy, or pranic, body to hold on to the physical body recedes. As the information runs out, life slowly peters out. Physical life begins to lose its intensity.

This is why you may notice that even a person who has lived a very base, material life often seems in the last few days before their death to carry an air of ethereal peace, maturity, and wisdom. Such a person is much less attached to people and less shaken by external situations.

When the pranic (energy) body is feeble, it will slip out of the body. This is what we call death by old age. The doctors invariably diagnose this as an organ failure of some sort, but the fact is just that the person has slipped out of the body because of the feebleness of the energy body. This is the ideal way to die because you are not being forced out of the body; you are naturally moving out. This is a good way to go.

However, how rapidly you empty your Allotted Karma depends on how swiftly you are willing to move from one aspect of life to another. If at eighty, you still think you should act as you did at eighteen, you are in trouble. You will die an unnatural death, because even if you live to be a hundred, your body will run down, but your karmic information will not.

Now, if a person's Allotted Karma is not worked out, but their body breaks for some reason—perhaps they crash their car or drink themselves to death or contract some fatal disease—their karma still remains. The same volume of Allotted Karma is still present, which means that the person's individuality is still strong. Such a disembodied being is in popular parlance termed a ghost. Their Allotted Karma and energy body is still intense, but there is no physical body to support it. The intellect and the discretionary capacity of the mind also goes at this point, but a bundle of tendencies, or vasanas, remains.

Such beings exist now not on the basis of discretion or conscious volition but on the basis of their tendencies, which buffet them about without any volition on their part. Since they are ruled only by tendencies at this point, the karma takes much longer to work itself out.

Basically, this means that if you function unconsciously, your karma rules you absolutely. As soon as you function with some awareness, the power of karma over your life weakens. In life beyond the body, discretion does not exist, so karma rules absolutely. If you have pleasant karma within you, it gets magnified, and if you have unpleasant karma within you, it gets intensified. It is these internal conditions that are referred to as heaven and hell in many traditions.

This is why it is so important to address your karma when you are in the embodied state. At this point, you can work out in ten years what might take a hundred years in the disembodied condition.

Even today, there are tendencies that are pushing and pulling you. This is why the word *responsibility* is so important. It is your responsibility to exercise the choice every moment of your life: either to follow your tendency or to make a conscious decision. If you live with this sense of responsibility, your tendencies will not rule you, and your future will not mimic the past.

There is much terror in the world around the idea of ghosts. Since the Allotted Karma is still strong, their presence is felt a little more strongly for a little while. The more sensitive may be able to sense this. But there is nothing to fear about their presence. Think of a ghost simply as a person, like you, who happened to lose their body. You are also a ghost, but *with* a body. Not much of a difference, really! A ghost with a body can cause much harm, as you know, but a ghost without a body has meager capabilities.

Karma and Memory Loss

Modern medicine has made it possible for us to live longer than a previous generation could have ever imagined. This is wonderful. However, to lengthen the life of the physical body without taking care of the karmic fiber is lopsided development. We now have a certain mastery over biochemistry and are capable of using medicine and surgery to prolong the life span. But the rub is that modern medicine knows nothing about karma.

This is one of the reasons for the upswing in the number of older people losing their mental faculties. The hardware is fortified and strengthened, but no software exists. This is like having a "dumb" computer, capable of existing in its materiality, but incapable of functioning.

The advances in medicine are not to be derided. Much has been achieved. However, without new karmic substance, the body is an empty shell. Even if you replace a heart, a kidney, hips, shoulders, elbows, and every other moving part in the body and create a new bionic individual, the human being cannot function without karma.

If our pursuit of external science and technology were accompanied by a pursuit of inner well-being, this would be less of an issue. But enhancing the physical without finding access to the nonphysical dimension is the fundamental problem.

Once you know how to open up the warehouse of Accumulated Karma (sanchita), you will actually be able to generate more than enough software. Even if your physical body were to endure for a thousand years, you would not lose your mind, because there would be software enough to sustain it.

If you cultivated the spiritual life, you would have another option, too. Once your software starts diminishing, you would have the freedom and balance to know when to shed your hardware. In other words, you would know when and how to walk out of the physical body. You would exit before you are evacuated.

Samadhi: Reaching the Summit

For the yogic practitioner, as the intensity of practice increases, the energies start moving upward. Now the contact with the physical body becomes minimal. If this goes beyond a certain point, the person attains what is known as samadhi.

Sama means equanimous, and *dhi* refers to the intellect. When you reach an absolutely equanimous state of intellect in which you are unable to distinguish between the concepts of *you* and *the other; this* and *that; here* and *there*, you have reached a state of samadhi. A mirror simply reflects everything. Nothing sticks to it; no residue is left upon it, and it never makes any judgment about what it reflects. It does not discriminate between pleasant and unpleasant, beautiful and ugly. When your mind becomes like this, you are in a state of samadhi. When all these distinctions drop away, the life energy no longer clings to the body. At this point, it starts dislodging itself from the physical.

If you remain in this condition for an extended period of time, you could well slip out of the body. This is why people in these conditions are kept protected in spiritual communities. This protection is necessary because the slightest jolt or pinprick to the system can make people in these states leave their physical bodies for good. They are so much on edge and their contact with the body is so fragile that this is a very real possibility.

While many have exited their body in such a state, other yogis want to root themselves in the body and still experience the freedom of not being in it. This balance was required when I needed to do a certain kind of energy work. In order to consecrate the Dhyanalinga, I needed people around me who could be intensely active and meditative at the same time. This is a rare combination because when energies are rooted in the body, you are fit for survival but not for transformation. When your energy contact with the body is minimal, you can transform rapidly, but survival is precarious.

What makes transformation so rapid when energy contact with the body is minimal?

Essentially, the fact that your energies become very fluid. Now you can take your life from one dimension to another with ease. It is like the earthen pot that I mentioned earlier: it becomes rigid once the clay is burned. Karma is similar. It is so deeply imprinted on the physiological, psychological, and energetic levels that it keeps manifesting itself in a million different ways. It has backup systems everywhere. So if you want to un-burn the earthen pot and make it a malleable ball of clay again, you have to do some intense energy work.

During the Dhyanalinga consecration, we had people whose physical contact was so minimal that it was almost like having pure clay again. Now the options are many: you can make ten pots into one big pot, or you can make twenty-five pots out of them! So when energies are so malleable and fluid that they are no longer stuck to one particular form, it allows for several transformational and creative possibilities.

For the yogi, the ultimate aim is *mahasamadhi,* or ultimate dissolution of the limited identity. This means a voluntary relinquishment of the physical, mental, and energy bodies. There is nothing life-denying about this. It is instead about giving up the limited for the unlimited. You could think of it like this: Instead of sitting on the beach, you choose to become the ocean. You choose to move from limited pleasure to the unfathomable ecstasy of boundless existence.

A yogi of great accomplishment will dissolve most of his karmic load, keeping a small volume that can be worked out just before his final exit. However, there are also yogis who walk the path of love and devotion—or *bhakti*, as it is called. Such people are able to leave through the sheer intensity of their emotion. Such people have not dissolved all their karma; indeed, their longing is itself a deep karma. The intensity of their emotion, however, enables them to distance themselves from their karma.

When such a person attains mahasamadhi, the karmic structure will endure for a while without any etheric or bliss body inside. It is like an empty shell. This karmic shell will fall apart in time, although it sometimes needs to be broken to hasten the process.

Avadhutas: Beings of Bliss

The purpose of yoga is to open up various spaces within you that are *not you*. Initially, this dimension of *not you* may be just a speck. Gradually, as you nurture it with practice or start clearing karmic debris, this space starts expanding. A day comes when this space occupies everything within you.

That is when we can say you have become truly meditative. You are now in a state of equanimity—of samadhi—when the dance of duality no longer touches you. You can play the external game if you want. Otherwise, internally, you are fine just as you are. You are not identified with the game of *me* and *you* anymore.

Those whose limited identifications have dropped away so completely that they are unable to function in the outside world are known as *avadhutas* in Sanskrit. Avadhutas are mystics who have journeyed so far beyond worldly consciousness that they turn utterly childlike. They are sometimes even perceived as crazy. They have dropped the intellect so completely that they do not know how to survive in the outside world and have to be looked after.

Such internal states may not last forever, but they do last for lengths of time, sometimes for years. These are blissful and wonderful states, but social situations need to be supportive for people in such conditions, because they cannot look after themselves. Traditionally, however, such people were celebrated in India. There have been avadhutas all over the country, wonderful beings who have been revered for centuries after their time.

For small periods of time, it is good for people to go into these states. It is a bit like sweeping the lowest floor of your karmic structure. It takes enormous awareness to reach so deep within yourself and undertake such cleaning. But in this kind of state, one can reach the bottom very easily. An avadhuta is in such a state of bliss that they have no karma, no bondage, and everything is naturally cleaned up for them. So yogis sometimes remain in such states for periods because it is the quickest path to liberation.

However, at the time of leaving the body, a yogi will emerge from this state. This is because it takes awareness to relinquish the body. The key thing is to leave the body in a state of consciousness, without creating further karma.

Retaining the Body After Bursting the Karmic Bubble

How do enlightened beings survive? Is it possible to retain the physical body after breaking the karmic bubble? Is it possible to live after burning up all one's karma?

It is, but it takes engineering. Since enlightened beings no longer have a karmic footprint, it is very difficult for them to retain a physical form. Yogis have various tricks to accomplish this. One option is to perform conscious karma to retain the body. Many mystics down the ages have done this. Otherwise, the temptation to leave the body is very strong once the karmic bubble has burst.

Different yogis have created different methods. Many have maintained some simple conscious attachments: either toward a spiritual mission or toward food. These are simple desires that they can drop at any time. Those around them have often been confounded by their behavior. How could someone so spiritually elevated be attached to something so worldly? But it is usually a conscious need to create karma in order to retain the physical body.

Soon after the consecration of the Dhyanalinga, my energy body was severely damaged. I had used it intensely and freely, and it was unfit to continue life in any way. Medically, I was a walking disaster. Lumps would manifest in different parts of my body, but ten days later they would be gone. I would go for a blood test one day, and doctors would diagnose various bizarre diseases. But a month later, there would be no evidence of these. I was doing my best to restore the energy body, but I also sought medical diagnoses to find out the extent of physical damage.

There is no way I could have sustained my life at this time had I not linked my energy body to the energy systems of some other beings. I seldom talk about the details because it would sound like some fairytale. But I mention this here to give you a sense of just how sophisticated the entire science of the energy body is.

Existentially, no distinction exists between the life of one being and that of another. But physically and mentally, there is, of course, separateness. By linking the two on an energy level, you can create a certain life support system for yourself. That is what I did until I fixed my physical body. It took me a long time, because I maintained a hectic work schedule through it all.

Mixing up one's life energies with those of others is a way of extending one's life or else of averting certain karmic events. In the first six months of 2005, for instance, it was clear to me that I would have a major injury in my right shoulder. This was not an injury that could be avoided by being careful. It was an inevitability. By mixing my energy body with those of others, however, I was able to confuse the karmic process, as it were, and avert it.

It is possible to extend the human form for a very long time if one knows how. The East is replete with stories of yogis who have lived for hundreds of years. These are dismissed as exaggerations today, but a very authentic arcane science of longevity makes this possible. The question, however, is, Why extend human life for no reason? It requires much manipulation of life energy, which incurs its own share of karma. It is not advisable to meddle with life on that level unless there is a specific purpose for it.

There is a well-known incident of a mystic who sat and meditated on the banks of the river Ganga in India. One day, there was a flood. He continued to meditate and was buried under the earth. Six months later, when cultivators were plowing the land, they accidentally hit his head. His head was wounded and started bleeding. Amazed, they dug farther and found the meditating yogi. He simply got up and walked away.

Now, this yogi was "hibernating" underground in an altered state of consciousness in order to extend his life. He knew his physical body had come to its end. At the same time, certain karmic bondages remained. He did not want to give up the physical body and return once more in another lifetime to work out his karma. So he decided to extend his life for a while so he could finish his Allotted Karma once and for all.

Systems of Energy Healing

Energy healing systems have grown very popular in the world today. My own take on them is unambiguous. While the intention to help others is a laudable one, it is juvenile to think that you can heal someone else because you have learned to harness a little energy in your hands.

What most people do not realize is that when you heal, you are only appeasing the karmic effect. You do not have the capability to take away the cause. If you merely remove the effect, the cause will take effect in some other way.

Let us say someone has asthma. That is their karma. As a healer, you lay your hands on them. You may be successful in removing the asthma. Now the asthma is gone, but the cause is not gone. It may manifest itself in some other way. It could become an accident or a heart attack. So do not ever seek to remove the effect. The effect is only an indicator of a problem; by merely erasing it, you are only enabling the seeds of the problem to manifest in some other way.

When there is pain in the body, for instance, it is an indicator that something is wrong. Pain is an opportunity to bring awareness to your system so you can investigate what is wrong. But if you simply pop a painkiller without attending to the cause, the mainspring of the ailment will keep growing, and one day it will strike even harder.

The only way to remove a cause is to take it upon your system. There was a time when I was doing this because the people I wanted to do some intense energy work with were stuck in certain cycles. Those two years, I was a very sick man. One day I would have an illness; the next day I would be completely healthy. One moment I would be all right; the next moment I would be so ill that people would think I was about to die. These fluctuations happened simply because I was throwing my life energy around liberally to create a certain basis for the work I was doing.

But today, it is only on rare occasions that I do this. I intervene only if I see that the person has dropped every identification and has only some small, niggling karmic issues left. This intervention is just to give them the needed push toward their destination. Otherwise, as a guru, I never interfere with the karmic process. I simply help hasten it.

I have pointed out the dangers of working with energy to any number of self-professed healers. Many who have looked closely at this work have given it up. Those for whom it is a lucrative livelihood have continued. If you are offering psychological solace to people, it is fine. But if you are healing people so that their ailments are actually going away, it is dangerous.

I invite healers to observe their patients. They will find that anywhere between six months to two and a half years, their patients will go through some other upheaval in their lives. It will not stop there. If the first upheaval hits them in the first eight months, the next will come within the next three years. If this second upheaval hits them within the next three years, the next will come within five and five and a half years. If you look out for the dates, you will see that these upheavals will occur with almost mathematical precision. But if the first upheaval hits them within three months, it will rapidly work itself out over the next three years.

There are various patterns to these upheavals. When I meet someone who is going through an upheaval right now, it is not difficult for me to know when it is going to hit them again. I do not predict doom for them, of course. Instead, I might say "Why don't you meditate?" Or "Why don't you do some hatha yoga?" If you do some spiritual practice, you can handle the problem from within and minimize its impact upon you.

You will also find that if you try healing others, within nine to eleven months much suffering will come to you. The suffering need not be in the form of physical calamities. It could be psychological as well. Now, if your attitude is one of absolute equanimity—"It doesn't matter to me, even if tragedies strike"— go ahead with your healing. But don't forget you are catalyzing calamities for the other person as well!

Also, what you might see as mere pain in someone else is also sometimes fuel to help them grow. It is unfortunate that many people lead frivolous and superficial lives until their lives are touched by pain. Do not think you are always helping them by alleviating it. Instead, help them go beyond it.

The ultimate guidance you can offer is to help someone transcend their suffering. This is what the great sages and mystics down the ages have done. They remind the world that there is a way out of suffering. Even if there is pain, there need be no suffering. The ability to see this difference is the supreme human attainment.

It may seem cruel, but it is actually the best thing that you can do for another. Why? Because you are offering them not temporary relief, but a permanent solution.

Many people who follow some spiritual practices gain small capabilities, such as the ability to heal or tell the future. But these are of no spiritual consequence. In the higher-level meditation programs I conduct, some people are able to acquire certain supernormal powers, or *siddhis,* as we call them in Sanskrit. However, as soon as I see these powers, I push them back immediately, even if doing so disturbs a person's trajectory of growth.

As a guru, I do not support siddhis. I destroy them. I am not interested in miracles. I put a halt to such capabilities right away because if a person acquires these powers, they will no longer pursue the spiritual path. They will set up their circus, try to make some money or acquire fame, and make a business out of it.

Do not try to become a franchisee for cosmic energy. And do not try to become a miracle worker. My only aim is to help you recognize the miracle of the life that you are. Everything else is a distraction.

SADHANA

It is important to remind yourself as often as possible that everything you consider to be yourself is an acquired identity.

One simple way to approach this realization is to make sure you are physically exhausted every night before you head off to bed. You will always sleep well and deeply. Many superfluous ideas about yourself will fall away, and so sleep of this kind can also be karmically rejuvenating.

But there is a more conscious exercise you could perform. Every night, sit on your bed, preferably cross-legged, with your eyes closed. Remind yourself that all memory is accumulation. Everything about you is acquired: your ideas of nationality, race, religion, all your relationships of like and dislike, love and hate.

Slowly, gently, start setting aside everything with which you have a relationship. This could mean setting aside people, as well as your material possessions. Remind yourself that even your body is an accumulation.

Imagine that you are on your deathbed and that you are going to die in two minutes. Put away everything that is not you—your sensations, thoughts, and emotions. See your sleep as impending death. You may feel a certain fear and struggle within you initially. But it will pass. Leave your body sitting and simply lie back with your eyes closed. Go to bed like this.

If you do this each night, a great deal of karma can be worked out each night. If you fall asleep as if you're dying, you will see that your karma barely has any impact on you. You will find over time that you are moving from compulsive behavior to a conscious existence.

You will be reborn daily.

PART THREE

PART THREE

◇◇◇

A Note to the Reader

This section is for those who have read the entire book but still have questions. Parts One and Two provide, I believe, a comprehensive exposition of karma. But I have been a guru long enough to know that questions have a way of surfacing at the close of a long journey.

This section is for those who have niggling doubts. It is also for those who wonder. If Parts One and Two addressed the *what* and *how* of karma, Part Three addresses the *buts* and *whys*. The mind has its questions: But how exactly does this work? But what really does that mean? The heart has its own questions, too: Why should this happen? Why is this so difficult to accept?

These are not the questions of nitpickers or the habitually suspicious. Karma is too closely related to the human condition to ever be just a mind game. These are instead the questions of genuine seekers, those who are still trying to absorb and internalize this material more deeply and fully.

No question is really new. Human beings have grappled with

variations of the same questions since the beginning of time. So you might well find several of your own queries and misgivings addressed in the following pages.

But if questions still linger after this section, that is all right, too. This book seeks to whet your appetite, not satiate it for good. It seeks to explore karma, not to offer ready-made conclusions. If you find questions still churning within you at the close of this book, it means only that it is time for some yoga. For it is in the laboratory of self-experiment that every question receives its own nonverbal answer.

And that is the deepest invitation at the heart of this book: an invitation to turn from reader to seeker.

◇◇◇

Karma Conversations

*As far as the laws of existence are concerned,
there is no good and bad, no crime and punishment.
It is just that for every action, there is a consequence.*

QUESTIONER: *Sadhguru, you say that our life is entirely of our making. But questions come up for which I have no answers. When I read a news report about a little girl being raped, for instance, can I really say that she deserved it because it is her karma?*

SADHGURU: Not her karma. Our karma.

QUESTIONER: *What does that mean?*

SADHGURU: It is our karma. Karma does not mean God is sitting up there punishing bad people and rewarding good ones. There is no such thing. But what kind of society we live in—is that not our collective karma? That we are living uninvolved in a society in which horrific things happen—is that not our karma? If all of us live without any humanity in our hearts for all the atrocities going on around us, that *is* our karma. We get the society we deserve. So don't think of it as her karma. Think of it as your own. Inaction is also karma.

You are asking this question because you read this disturbing news report. But if you have a little girl in your house, aren't you doing everything possible to make sure she is protected? Does that mean her safety is guaranteed? No, but you do your best to secure her protection. This is what we need to do for the entire society, for every little girl, wherever she is. And it is not impossible. In many ways, we have taken our collective destiny into our hands.

Take a simple example. When there are floods in India during the monsoons, people now demand accountability from their respective municipal corporations. This is because they see the floods as their collective karma, not merely an act of God. They want the necessary action to be taken to safeguard the security of all citizens.

Take another example. In 1947, the average life expectancy in India was twenty-eight years. Today, it is seventy-four. The reason we live longer today is because some action has been taken. Society and the nation have done something to improve life expectancy in the country. Is this not our collective karma? So steps have been taken for which we can be happy.

There are other areas that have not been adequately attended to in the world, like the safety of women and children, as you mention, for which we are also collectively responsible. If there is collective will, we can bring many things to some sense of order. With concerted and participatory action, much can be changed. But if you attribute all this to divine will, things will go on endlessly in the same way.

It doesn't matter whether you can perceive how you shaped your collective karma or not. Just see yourself as the creator of your karma. If you see that this is your karmic web, that this is your doing, the next moment will naturally be conscious. If you attribute your fortune to someone else, you will act only unconsciously. But if you see yourself as the creator of your karma, it will shape the way you think, feel, and act. And you now realize you have the power to affect the lives of many, many others around you.

But remember this: for every thought that you generate, there is a consequence. Don't ever try to fix the consequence. The consequence will happen anyway. It is not something you can control. But the process is your doing. If you manage the process well, the consequence will be good. You can be sure of that.

QUESTIONER: *I have a friend who has lost his legs because he was affected by polio at birth. What kind of past karma could cause such a terrible consequence?*

SADHGURU: You're making the mistake again of interpreting karma as a system of reward and punishment. The first step is to see it as software. Nothing more.

Now, a hundred years ago, there were any number of polio-affected children and adults everywhere in the world, but today those numbers have reduced dramatically because we are doing the right karma. What is the right karma? We are vaccinating our children. It is unfortunate that we did not know the importance of this earlier, but this ignorance was also our collective karma. It is good that we are doing something about it now.

As far as the laws of existence are concerned, there is no good and bad, no crime and punishment. It is just that for every action, there is a consequence. Actions may happen knowingly or unknowingly. So when you perform any action, only one question is relevant: Are you ready for the consequence? If you can joyfully accept any consequence, do whatever you please. But if the consequences matter to you, you must perform conscious action.

Now, suppose you were driving with a drunk friend. If he crashes his car, you might also be seriously injured. If you were to say "This is unfair—this is his karma, not mine," it would be absurd. Your karma is that you were with a drunken friend. This is the way existence works. If you are in tune with it, it will not crush you. If you are not in tune with it, it will crush you.

Now, maybe you lost your legs because you were ignorant of polio, or you were with a drunk friend who happened to be driving, or you were ignorant of gravity and you were on the roof and you just walked off. The scenarios are different, but the consequence is basically due to your being in the wrong place at that given moment. How do any of us catch an infection? Simply by being in the wrong environment. Or, anyway, an environment that's right for the virus and wrong for us!

Now, why are some people in the wrong place and some not? This may sound cruel and capricious to you, but this is the way life works. You may be a wonderful person, a great philanthropist, much loved by your family and friends, but today if you went and ate the wrong food, you will still get an infection. It will not spare you because you are a good man. It is time to stop thinking of good and bad. We urgently need sensible people on this planet now—people who will do the right thing with life. People who operate on the basis of *life sense*.

We did not know many things about illness in the past. We did not know how we contracted many diseases or how to treat them, whether it was cholera, plague, or polio. Slowly, we have understood how to tackle them, but there are still other diseases we do not know how to handle. It is sad that many people have already paid the price for our ignorance. But at least we are doing something to alter our collective karma.

Now, without trivializing your friend's condition in any way, I want you to see that advantage and disadvantage are only by comparison. Suppose none of us had legs—we would all be crawling around quite okay. It is because most people have legs that we believe that one who doesn't will suffer. If no one had eyes, we would not consider blindness a problem. But now comparing oneself to someone else is the problem. And that is the karma.

It is time we stopped focusing on disadvantage. Can all of us perform the same type of physical and mental activity? No. Someone can do more, and someone less. Even with legs, most people cannot run. So, socially, if we create a situation that does not set up discrimination or an atmosphere that is not overly dripping with sentimental pity, there would be no problem. If you treat your friend as you would treat yourself, he would be fine. Don't treat him with any self-conscious sympathy because you see him as an object of pity. Physically, he cannot do a few things; you can help him with those. For the rest of it, just treat him as you would any other human being.

Society needs to be mature enough to deal with those with disabilities. If they are treated as normal, their suffering will disappear because their suffering is not physical. Pain is physical, but suffering is entirely psychological. Now, you could sit at home right now and weep because you cannot play soccer like Ronaldinho! You could consider yourself disadvantaged and handicapped. But it is foolish to do this—either to yourself or to another person. Offer some physical assistance to those who need it, but do not overexaggerate their problem and make them feel like a victim.

SUTRA #11

*When there is no imprint of karma in conscious experience,
every action and experience becomes liberating.*

QUESTIONER: *Does karma presuppose past lives, Sadhguru? Do I
have to believe in rebirth in order to understand karma?*

SADHGURU: No, it is not necessary. Never mind if somebody else
is talking about past lifetimes. When you're looking at your
karma, just look at those areas of bondage that are a reality for
you. Start from where your experience begins. You can start only
from where you are. Efforts to start with something that is not
in your experience will lead to hallucinatory states.

From the moment of your birth to the present moment,
examine the very way you think and feel. At least since your
birth, you can see your past actions have been ruling you in so
many ways. And the very way you think, feel, understand, and
express yourself now will affect your future.

Let us not talk about those things that are not in your realm
of experience. Otherwise, your entire life could pass in self-
deception. These deceptions could make you a popular conversa-
tionalist at a dinner party. They may carry you across one evening,
but they won't carry you across life and death!

If I tell you about your past lives, I am merely giving you a
story, a belief, not an experience. A belief system will not offer
you growth; it offers you only solace or entertainment. If I tell
you that God will look after you, it will offer you only solace.
Solace is like a tranquilizer; it means you are only getting deeper
into entanglement. It will not liberate you.

Right now, you are not able to handle the memory of this

very lifetime. You still suffer what happened to you ten years ago! When you are in this condition, if you remember what happened to you ten lifetimes ago, it will drive you nuts! So there is no point speculating about earlier lifetimes. At the same time, don't dismiss the idea either. You can simply acknowledge that you don't know.

For now, you could simply see whatever you call "past life" as unconscious layers of memory in the mind. If you meditate and attain heightened levels of awareness, these unconscious layers of the mind that are ruling you from within could be broken down, dissolved.

Gautama the Buddha described his lifetimes in great detail—including all his animal lives, right down to the state of a single-celled organism. His description parallels Darwin's theory of evolution in many ways. Now, you could see this as a journey into the deepest layers of the unconscious mind. Gautama could access all this within his consciousness, without the help of a microscope, simply because he turned inward. Countless yogis have done this.

On the level of information, it will not help you to know anything about your past lives. But on a deeper energy level, undergoing previous experiences can help. What looking into the past can do is to help you arrive at a deeper understanding of what makes up the person you call "myself."

There are layers and layers of memory in the unconscious. Karma Samyama, an advanced spiritual program we do at Isha, is a meditation that brings layers of the unconscious mind to the surface to dissolve them. Anything that is karmic dissolves only when the discerning mind is in function. If you just leave it unexamined, it hardens into a tendency. These tendencies are working upon you all the time.

I know today there is a big psychological circus going on in the form of past-life regressions. Much of this is pure hallucination. You need to understand that this mind is an incredible instrument. It can deceive you in many subtle ways. Suppose you realized your neighbor's dog was your husband in your previous life, how would it help you? Whether you now go and kiss him or throw stones at him doesn't matter. Both are dangerous! (If you throw stones at him, you will get into trouble with the neighbor. If you kiss him, you will get in trouble with the dog!)

But on a different plane, if you can bring this memory into your experience, then it becomes a way of liberating yourself. In Samyama, no suggestions are given to you; no guidance is given to you. But the process allows layers and layers of the past to surface and work themselves out by moving you to a certain level of intense awareness. You are now free of several impulses and tendencies.

The other advantage of a process like this is that it can break some of your illusions. Right now, you consider your life to be your home, your spouse, your children, your work. But suppose you looked more deeply and saw that you had gone through many lifetimes, many spouses, dozens of children, enacted the same old charades—the same anger, the same jealousy, the same hatred, the same ambitions, the same foolishness—and died frustrated each time. Once you have a clear vision of this, your present illusions can be dismantled very easily. Any amount of teaching cannot accomplish this. Just looking into the past can make you feel absolutely stupid. The more you have seen something, the less fascinating it becomes. If you see that you have enacted the same patterns again and again, they become less compelling.

If you look back on dozens of lives, you will have no urge to go through the same nonsense again and again. Once you know that the mortal way is just a repetition, you will seek another way—the eternal way. No one really wants to keep repeating the same rigmarole time and again. Few are that foolish; most people are just forgetful.

The problem is that when you undergo experiences unconsciously, you do not learn from them. It does not matter how many times it happens: if you keep forgetting, you will repeat the same actions. If it is a conscious experience, however, it will always transform you. In Samyama, you do not work out your karma on the level of memory, but on the level of conscious energy experience.

Even now, your personality is a projection of many past lives. But this is an unconscious projection. If this becomes a conscious projection, you will see that the anger or jealousy you are experiencing right now will be transformed into love and compassion. If you see that your rage and resistance are only because of past influences, they will transform instantly into something positive. It is because you cannot see that your present personality is just a projection of the past that you cling to it.

Once it happened.

A seventy-year-old man who had great fear of flying gathered all his courage and decided to take a flight. He flew on a small aircraft. Once they landed, he went up to the pilot with a flushed face and thanked him.

"I want to thank you for both trips," he said gratefully.

"What do you mean, both trips?" asked the pilot. "You flew only once."

"No, no, I flew twice," said the passenger. "This was my first and last trip!"

Experience is like this. In experiencing consciously, there is no imprint of karma. Every experience and action becomes liberating. Once you have tasted something consciously, there is no need to keep revisiting it. That aspect of karma is finished.

QUESTIONER: *So assuming previous lifetimes exist, how does the machinery work? Does the child select its parents? Or do the parents determine the karmic inheritance of their child?*

SADHGURU: Yes, the child selects the parents. But selection does not mean that the child chooses consciously. It is like this: If we let a whole group of people into a hall, each one goes and finds their own place. The reason you choose a particular place is your karma. If your karma is back pain, you go and settle next to a wall at the back. If your karma is that of the student who always liked to hide in class, you may choose to sit behind a big person. If your karma is about wanting to be noticed, you may choose the front row. These decisions may be unconscious, but they do operate.

Similarly, your karma makes you settle down in a particular womb. In other words, you choose an environment with which you may share tendencies or attributes. It is not that two people are named as parents for you. That is not how it works. It is just a plug waiting for a suitable socket. Once it finds the appropriate place with certain similarities or affinities, it settles down there. That is all.

This is why elaborate care was taken in traditional India over arrangements and rituals around conception. To some degree, a few simple rituals still prevail. For every wedding, an auspicious date was chosen, because that night was the night when the woman would conceive. So the right time of the month was fixed and a pleasant atmosphere and energetic situation created so that the conception happened in the best possible conditions. This was both for the woman and for the new life that was being created within her. If conception happened in a certain state of love and joy, it would naturally attract a certain type of life. If it happened in a state of unpleasantness, it would attract another type of life. Of course, this happened in a traditional context when the couple in question was young. Today, no such social arrangement is possible, but couples can still arrange a situation of great pleasantness and energetic aliveness for themselves to ensure that they produce a better next generation.

Now, we cannot generalize on these matters. This does not mean that happy conditions will produce only a happy child. A mango can attract a fly. But the same fly is also attracted to a lump of shit. Karmic attraction can work in different ways. Sometimes a disturbed state of mind may attract a beautiful being because one type of personality might be drawn to its opposite. So don't start judging the kind of person you are based on your children. A child may be wonderful in spite of you!

But, essentially, tendencies drive a child to a particular womb. And because the child comes to you in such a tender state, you have the capability to influence them to a great extent. You can enhance either their pleasantness or their unpleasantness.

You don't have total control, of course. Nobody has complete control over another. With children, the less you try to influence them, the more they are influenced by you. The more you try to influence them, the less successful you will be.

Now, it is because of karma that even an unborn child has a certain nascent personality. If you ask women who have had more than two or three children, they will tell you that every child did not behave in the same way in the womb. The basis or the seed of the personality is already present. This is what we refer to as karma. The karmic body is already present in its entirety in the prenatal stage. By the time the child is born, it has as much of a karmic body as you have. It is only that the physical body has not yet filled out.

However, this does not mean that the child is at the mercy of their parents' karma. Certain choices still exist. Let's say your father was a criminal. Now, you have the choice to follow in his footsteps and become one; or if you have the awareness and intelligence, you might exercise the choice to opt for another kind of life. The genes may be the same, the environment may be ridden with crime, but some will still grow beyond it. Once there is a certain distance between you and all that you have gathered, you can make anything of your life. Once there is distance between you and your karma, you are free.

SUTRA #12

You cannot own life; you can only live it.

QUESTIONER: *You've said that after death, one operates only according to one's tendencies. This means working out karma in such a state will take a long time. But is it possible to work it out in the disembodied state, or does one have to take on another body and enter the human form again?*

SADHGURU: The question you're asking is like this: "I was driving my car and I fell asleep. In my sleep, can I still go where I want to go?" Of course, you will go, but go where? Because that's the nature of unconsciousness. When you're unconscious, where you go is not your choice. Even a dead leaf goes somewhere, but where? It cannot decide. The wind will decide. Even a little ant knows where exactly it wants to go, but any being that's become totally unconscious cannot choose. Once you have lost the discerning part of your mind, you have no choice. Whichever way the tendencies push you, that's where you will go.

Now, your question is, "Can I undo my karmic stuff in the disembodied state?" I thought you were planning to do it here when you're still alive! Why do you want to do it after you lose your body and lose discernment? The most important dimension of your existence right now is that you have a discerning mind.

If you have any sense, you will choose what is best for this life. That is the most important thing. Will you use your discernment to make this into the most wonderful life there is? This is the only question that counts.

But, yes, when you make choices out of awareness and discernment, then undoing your karma is very rapid. When you don't have a discerning mind, some aspects will continue to be undone because of the natural process of evolution. But the whole process is inordinately slow.

It happened.

A man got an appointment with God. He asked God, "Father, is it true that what is a billion dollars for us in America is just a penny for you? And is it true that what is a million years for us is just a second or moment for you?"

God said, "Yes, my son, that's how it is. That is the proportion between where you live and where I live."

The man said, "My father, just so I can always remember you, would you give me a penny?"

God said, "Just wait a moment."

So that's the scale we're talking about! Don't even think of unwinding karma in the disembodied state. When you're unconscious, when you've lost your faculties, a minuscule amount of karma may be undone. But that's not important. It should not even be thought of.

There are traditions, including the yogic one, in which if one has done substantial inner work and some small amount remains undone, some external assistance will be given after one loses the body. Outside help is offered to break the karmic bondage.

Now, the next question from some people will inevitably be "Sadhguru, if I stop doing all my practices, will you take care of me after I'm dead?"

So don't forget, I said *if* substantial inner work is done and only a little karma is left! Don't concern yourself with what happens to you after you die. If you wish to assist others who have died, there are certain dimensions and possibilities of sadhana that I will be opening up in the coming years so we can genuinely do something to help those who are in the disembodied state.

QUESTIONER: *What happens to beings who have died when their energy body is still vibrant?*

SADHGURU: If the pranic or energy body is still vibrant, such a being cannot find another body for some time. The energy body needs to settle down. This is why those who die in an accident, or suicide, or who contract some sudden illness sometimes linger on in a disembodied state. Such a pranic body still carries desires, longings, strong inclinations. These have to run their course. It is a limbo condition, and traditionally in India several rituals were performed to hasten the course of such a being. Some of these rituals were just about psychological solace for the living. But even today, if these rituals are performed by those who know what they are doing, they can accelerate the process for such a being.

People long to die peacefully for this reason: The prana or life energy has run its full course and can easily disentangle itself. It is like a ripe fruit falling off a tree. The moment it falls, with the ripe fruit around it, the seed will immediately take root with the necessary food around it. See, the seed has the necessary manure around it; a fruit is actually manure for the seed—we just happen to eat it before it actually becomes manure! Another function of the fruit is to attract animals and insects so that they will carry it elsewhere and drop it in places where it can take root again. So when people die after a full life cycle, they fall without a struggle, disease, or injury. The prana reaches a certain level of sedateness and disentangles itself.

Now what we call *mahasamadhi* is the reverse: to bring the prana to a certain state of intensity and maturity in the structure so that it cannot be held in the physical form anymore. The reason yogis seek such a death is because it is natural, effortless. If you die with a disease or accident, there is violence in the death. The residual impact of that violence endures in so many ways in the subtle body.

Now, you may wonder, Does time exist for the disembodied being? Yes, there is cyclical time in the disembodied state, but not in the way we understand it here. If the energy body is in a state of great pleasantness, there may be no urgency to take on a physical embodiment again. If it is restless, the urgency is greater. Think of it in terms of your own life. If you are depressed, one minute feels like a day. If you are joyful, one day is like a minute. For a suffering energy body, a single day may seem like a hundred years; but for a joyful one, a hundred years could seem like a day.

So for those who have died without living out a full life cycle, the Allotted Karma, or prarabdha, has to wear itself out. The pranic body has to come to a certain state of passivity or inertness. This happens when there is no longer any active karmic substance. Now, the new allotment, or installment of prarabdha, will begin to manifest itself. As this happens, the energy body regains its vibrancy and will then take on another physical body.

QUESTIONER: *Does anyone ever manage to work out their Accumulated Karma, or sanchita, in a single lifetime? If one keeps accumulating karma even as one sheds it, it seems like an endless process!*
SADHGURU: For the enlightened being, as I said before, the challenge is about how to *accumulate* karma. For the enlightened being, it is like this: You make sure you don't burn up all your karma. You burn down your warehouse to one sack. Then when you see you have no way to live, you carry a handbag for today's

expense! You create a purpose and then work it out. That is the strategy for the enlightened being.

But for the seeker, I would say: Don't worry about getting rid of karma. Just concern yourself with how not to acquire new karma. This anxiety—"I want to get rid of my karma"—will itself breed more karma. So don't get caught up with how to burn it all up. Karma will melt down with the process of life itself; living is itself burning karma.

Karma is not some kind of punishment. It is just information. How you carry your information will determine whether it becomes burdensome, restrictive, painful, joyful, or liberating. It all depends on how you carry it. Nowadays, your phone alone doesn't carry all your memory; an entire cloud follows you around everywhere. If you learn to carry your karma like this, it's good. If your karma follows you but doesn't sit on your head, what does it matter? You aren't burdened, so the bigger the cloud, the better. Having more gigabytes is always better, isn't it?

Now, how do you not gather karma? As we've seen, the simplest thing you can do is to make your involvement absolute, not selective. The air that you breathe, the sound you hear, the ground you sit on—be absolutely involved with all of it. Unbridled involvement is the nature of life itself. The tree standing here is involved with everything—the earth, the water, the breeze, the sky, everything. Life will blossom only if involvement is total. Once you discriminate, karma multiplies big-time.

This is what every human being should aspire to: discrimination only on the level of action, not involvement. Action is necessarily limited. It involves a certain expenditure of energy, time, competence, and other factors. Discretion is necessary only on the level of action; otherwise, you will waste yourself. But involvement is an internal state, and it needs to be all-inclusive.

Ideas based on selectivity—"this is my house," "this is my

work," "this is my country"—are relevant only on the level of external behavior and action. It is a fact that you cannot physically give birth to all the people on this planet. But, internally, you can be as involved as you would be with your own children. You may not be able to feed or educate every child, but you can still be involved wholeheartedly with all of creation. The moment you try to curtail and concretize this natural movement of life that is constantly trying to evolve and burst forth, you turn into a monument!

Life cannot be owned. The need to own life is responsible for much suffering on this planet. Let's say you meet someone and say "I love you." It feels really nice for three days. Then you think you must capture this love. Well, you ended up with a marriage! Nothing wrong with that. But the beauty of an experience cannot be captured; it cannot be institutionalized. This is the fundamental reason karma has become a problem. It is because you're trying to capture life. You cannot own life; you can only live it.

SUTRA #13

Right now, you are like a bubble that says "The air that I hold in my lungs is my air." You still have to exhale!

QUESTIONER: *I have always wondered about this: If there are a certain number of beings that need to be liberated from their karma, why is the human population always increasing? Where is all the new karmic substance coming from?*

SADHGURU: The number game works only with the physical dimension. In the nonphysical dimension, it is meaningless. You are confusing the nonphysical dimension with the physical.

With a single person's karmic body, it is possible to make a million children! This does not mean a million people have to die and a million women have to get pregnant and wait to receive those million beings. A single karmic body can manifest in a million wombs.

So this being that you call "me" right now is not a quantity. I always use negative terminology so your imagination doesn't fly away with you. Let me just describe this "you" as empty space or darkness. (If I describe you as light or as God, you will start turning hallucinatory. If I tell you that you are light, you will immediately tell your neighbor that you are divine light. If I tell you that you are God, you will start turning delusional. There is not very much you can imagine about emptiness, so let's stick with that description.)

So this empty space within you is like a bubble. Karma is the wall of the bubble. Without karmic substance, you have no existence. It is only because of karmic substance that you are glued to the body. If all your karma is removed, you cannot be held in the body. Even though you may slip out of one physical body, the karmic substance is still there. So even if this body loses its vibrancy, the karmic substance will find another body.

Now, when we say we want liberation, or *mukti*, what we really are saying is that we want to prick this bubble in such a way that the enclosed emptiness becomes one with the emptiness outside. Once you burst a bubble, the air inside becomes part of everything around it, doesn't it? It works the same way with the karmic bubble. Enlightenment also means the same thing: it means the bubble has burst. For most beings, the moment of enlightenment and the moment of leaving the body are the same. Only a few who know the tricks of the body—its fundamental mechanics—are able to retain the physical for a length of time after their enlightenment.

Now, if life energies become overly intense, you cannot

retain the body. Also, if life energies become very feeble, you cannot retain the body. So only if life energies are within a certain bandwidth of intensity can the body be retained. This is why there are two types of yoga in the world. One type is about withdrawing from the world. This means making the life energies so feeble that you can drop the body. Another type of yoga is about revving up the energies to a high pitch so that the physical cannot hold one anymore. Socially, the revving-up approach may be more appreciated. But, existentially, one is not superior to the other. Both achieve the same end.

So there is no such thing as "you" and "me," really. Right now, you are like a bubble that says, "The air that I hold in my lungs is *my* air." But you still have to exhale! When you do, your air becomes somebody's else's air, and somebody else's air becomes your air. There is no such thing as "my air," but when you hold it in your lungs, it becomes you for that little period of time. So that limited aspect of the divine that you hold within you, you call your soul. In Sanskrit, we call it *atma*. We differentiate it from the divine, which we call *paramatma*.

If the bubble breaks, it's all paramatma. Even now, it is all paramatma, but we speak of the soul, or atma, because we like to believe that the air in our lungs is "ours" and the food in our stomachs is "ours." We believe our flesh, blood, and bone are "ours," and even "us." In fact, atma, or soul, is just an imaginary creation. It is true in your current context, but, existentially, it is not. In truth, there is only paramatma. But we end up fighting over "my" divinity and "your" divinity, "my" air and "your" air.

So a single person's karmic body can be made into a million children. The same karma can be worked out through several beings. There is no fixed arithmetic as far as souls are concerned. Atma is our own creation. It is relevant only in a limited subjective context.

This can happen, and has, in fact, happened in the past. Let us say that my body has become defunct and I am unable to sustain it. I have to leave it, but I am in a hurry to complete some unfinished work that might perhaps take me five more years. I may not want to go through a womb, be born, grow up, maybe get lost again, and have to do sadhana to find my way back again to my central mission. So I might choose to find a suitable adult body that is going to be discarded by someone else, and inhabit it. This means I can complete my unfinished business.

The karmic material can definitely take on more than one body. It is capable of supporting more than one physical form. I have spoken in the past of how this happened with me in an earlier lifetime. When I was Sadhguru Sri Brahma and life situations made it impossible for me to continue my mission to consecrate the Dhyanalinga, I took on the body of a child yogi who had left his body early. For a while, I managed two bodies and made a futile attempt to consecrate the Dhyanalinga. I attempted this because I knew that the physical term for that body, as Sadhguru Sri Brahma, was going to be over in a few months.

The tradition also has stories of other yogis who maintained two different bodies to fulfill two different kinds of karma. There were yogis who inhabited the body of an ascetic and a house-holder, in order to fulfill certain dimensions of activity that could not be carried out with a single body. There have also been cases of two yogis sharing a single body. It is sometimes simpler to share another yogi's body and fulfill one's karmic obligations rather than go through the process of finding a womb and starting over.

QUESTIONER: *Will the million children produced from the same karmic body be similar?*

SADHGURU: Not necessarily. There are many other factors at work, too: genetic influences, family influences, social influences. The karmic body represents only a certain amount of information. The rest comes from parents, education, society, cultural environment, and a host of other factors. So it does not mean that the karmic body will always manifest as the same type of human being.

SUTRA #14

In maintaining distance from
your thought and emotion,
you can become available to the grace of
the greatest beings of the past.

QUESTIONER: *What exactly do you mean by collective karma? How does individual karma intersect with collective karma?*

SADHGURU: The problem is that you are thinking again in terms of the individual as separate from everything else. There is no such thing.

Today, psychologists speak of that aspect of the individual unconscious that is connected with a larger collective unconscious. This is what we mean by collective karma. Because we perform certain actions, karma accumulates. This has individual and collective consequences.

Imagine a pond full of water. You go there and scoop out a bucketful of water. Then you scoop out another. Is the first bucketful any different from the second? Can you speak of "this" water and "that" water? It is the same with life. You cannot speak of "this" life and "that" life.

At this moment, if you are willing, the karma of Adiyogi, the first yogi and first guru, can become yours. It has already become ours in so many ways. There are so many things he achieved through his karma that we are making use of today. It has become our karma. You may never have gone through the sadhana he underwent, but you can enjoy the fruits of his karma because it is simply there, available to all.

This means that Adiyogi's karma is large enough to accommodate many other beings. This is why so many realized beings have performed action. They do not need to. Action is no longer needed for them. But they perform it in order to produce more positive karma. Rather than a single yogi, ten can come with the same karma. This is a tremendous possibility.

Do not think of action as belonging to a particular person. Every thought that you generate finds a certain imprint in this universe forever and ever. Every thought that ever occurred to Adiyogi, every thought that ever occurred to Krishna or the Buddha—all this still has a presence. Now, if you create the right kind of situation within yourself, you can access this karma. You could receive Adiyogi's thoughts, or if you create another kind of situation, you could receive the Buddha's thoughts. In other words, their karma is becoming your karma. In maintaining distance from your thought and emotion, you can become available to the grace of the greatest beings of the past.

But do not think that you can perform any action you choose and still gather someone else's good karma for yourself. There has been a great emphasis in the yogic tradition on cultivating the right attitude toward life because, depending on your attitude or quality, you attract that kind of thought, emotion, and experience toward yourself.

Why has there been so much talk of God? Or in the yogic tradition, why is there no mention of God, but only of the ultimate guru, Adiyogi, or the first yogi? It is only because this helps you become the right kind of receptacle. Although you are not able to become spiritual by effort, by enhancing your receptivity, you will slowly draw the right thoughts, the right emotions, the right feelings, the right blessings toward you. It will definitely happen. So karma does not belong to a person alone. It exists, and it can be attracted, depending on your receptivity.

So all the karma you carry is not actually "your" karma in some narrowly individual sense. Because of the karma that you have performed, you have attracted this kind of karma to yourself in this lifetime. This is the significance of the tradition of sending a child to a guru at an early age. The abode of the guru was called *gurukula*—literally, the guru's family. The guru's karma was seen as so good that spending time with him was a way of downloading some of his karma. The child might belong to any family, but going to a gurukula meant you became part of the guru's clan. What was his became yours. Learnings that might have taken lifetimes became yours, too. Your life was put on fast-forward, which accelerated your inner evolution.

The reason there is so much emphasis in the tradition on creating good karma is just this. If you generate a lot of good karma in the world, the new generation will be born with better karma. The situation of the world will now automatically improve. Those new beings who catch this karma and come into the world will, in turn, attract more positive karma and generate more as well.

So don't think of quantities. Once your consciousness rises beyond this sense of separateness, where are the quantities? There are none. There is only one. And it is not even entirely correct to say there is one. When ten does not exist, one does not exist either. Since language is itself rooted in duality, we cannot escape the quantifying process. But the truth is that there is no "one" and no "two." This cannot be understood. It can only be experienced.

So there is just one common karma, because there is only one common existence. But based on your quality, you attract a particular kind of karma to yourself. The moment of death is particularly important in determining the kind of quality you have and the kind of karma you attract. So if you die in anger, in hatred, in misery or in pain, you attract one kind of karma. If you die in peace or blissfulness, you attract another kind of karma.

In the last forty seconds of a person's lifetime, many lifetimes of Accumulated Karma play out in fast-forward. In those crucial forty seconds, if a person manages to stay aware, they can drop lifetimes of karma. It does not matter what kind of life they have lived. If they are in a consecrated space, or if they have done some spiritual practice and manage to stay conscious, that intense phase will wipe them clean and they can dissolve their karma altogether.

This is why every religious tradition places an emphasis on dying in peace. This is simply because this gives one a better opportunity the next time round. Dying in joy or love is a wonderful way to die. Dying in what the yogic tradition calls the samadhi state is the ultimate way to die. This means that while you are living, you walk consciously into death.

SUTRA #15

You have the choice and ability to be any way you want in a given moment. That is the freedom and the curse. Most human beings are suffering their freedom.

QUESTIONER: *What about animals? Do they have karma, too?*
SADHGURU: Yes, animals have karma, but it is very limited and different from human karma. An animal lives an instinctive life.

This is the only difference between a human being and an animal. Only when you exercise your intelligence is a distinction set up between you and an animal. So when you live by your instincts, you accumulate karma but in a very limited way. When you employ your intelligence, suddenly the karma acquires a different significance.

An ant creates karma, but all ants create the same type of karma. There are no differences between their karmas, because there is no difference in their desire. Their desire is to eat, procreate, and protect themselves. They want to eat the dead cockroach in your home, and they want to make sure you don't step on them! So desire and fear immediately create a karmic structure. But it is a simple one. The structure becomes very complicated and intricate only when life becomes human, because now you create karma with volition. Simple karma can just be snapped and discarded. When there is conscious volition, karma gets very complicated.

For an animal, whatever happened to it in the past is recorded. If it dies a violent death, that gets recorded. Because of this, there may be a certain fear in the animal. But the karma does not manifest itself as dominantly as it does in a human being. When there is the freedom to decide how to be, karma gets more complicated. Tigers have no real choice other than to be a tiger. They go by their instincts. They have no choices as we know them: they cannot transform themselves into vegetarians or get married or become yogis! Their life is fixed, so there is not much karmic action. Certain personality differences still exist: there are angry tigers, docile tigers, lazy tigers. But there are no major differences. Human life, on the other hand, is not fixed. You have the choice and the ability to be any way you want in a given moment. That is the freedom and the curse. Most human beings are suffering their freedom.

SUTRA #16

Every human being is in the process of becoming divine. . . .
Collaborating with Nature's plan is all you need to do.

QUESTIONER: *So how does an animal evolve on the karmic ladder?*
SADHGURU: Life evolves by its own nature. Nature takes care of it. From the lower animals to the higher, from single-celled organisms to those with a central nervous system, the evolutionary journey just happens. It is not a choice. Because everything is unconscious and instinctual for animals, there is no good and bad, no right and wrong for them. Nature is just giving them a free ride! They move effortlessly from one grade of life to the other. It is just the flow of life itself. And at a certain point, the animal attains the human form. Now, as a human being, you have the freedom to decide your destiny; Nature no longer decides it for you.

The human problem right now is freedom! That is the paradox. You are free now to make yourself miserable; you are free to make yourself joyous. You are free to live like a god; you are free to live like a demon. Nature gave you freedom because you are now evolved enough to make a mature choice. In short, Nature trusted your intelligence. But unfortunately, human beings take their own time to make use of that intelligence.

Every human being is in the process of becoming divine. Every human being is in the process of awakening to their own divinity. Whether this happens today, tomorrow, ten years or ten thousand years later, is always open to question. But once you see that life is moving toward its ultimate nature of its own accord, you also put your energies into it and go faster. That is, you turn consciously spiritual. Collaborating with Nature's plan is all you need to do.

Existence is not in a hurry. But if you are, you could join hands with existence and reach your goal much more quickly. But if you're enjoying fooling around here, go right ahead. Existence is eternal, so you have all of eternity before you! There is no hurry. The choice is yours.

Every spiritual process is about transforming the animal nature within you. As you move toward a divine possibility, you must take care of your animal nature with the right kind of awareness and inner work. Merely pretending to be moral won't do. Many human beings who project themselves as very principled and upright find themselves consumed by their animal impulses—whether lust or greed—later in their lives. They completely lose their grip over themselves in their later years. So dissolving the animal nature is the aim of a daily spiritual process.

QUESTIONER: *Can a human being return to the animal stage in another lifetime?*

SADHGURU: No. However, some yogis may take on an animal form just to dissolve earlier karma. Others manage the animal stage in this life itself. Maybe someone is a yogi in this life. But for all their spiritual attainments, food remains a compulsion. So it is possible that they may choose not to return as a human being (which has its own complex entanglements). They may choose to return as an animal, just to work out the simple food karma. Now they don't get entangled with all the other processes of growing up human. And as an animal, which is a simpler form, they gather minimal karma. This makes it easy to break their food karma and not accumulate any other unwanted entanglements. Once this karma has been worked out, the same life returns as a much more accomplished human being. But the karma must be really base for a being to take on an animal form.

There have been stories about the twentieth-century Indian mystic Ramana Maharshi and how he granted mukti, or liberation, to a cow. Now, this is possible only if the animal is already a spiritually sophisticated being that is simply tenanting an animal body. Such an animal may find itself unconsciously drawn to the presence of a yogi like Ramana. Or else, it is possible for a yogi to take on another being's karma in their own body and in a single moment dissolve that life and release it. This means the cow leaves the body; the yogi then takes that life on his body for just a moment and liberates it. These are rare occurrences, however. They are not impossible, but they are rare.

There have been instances of spiritual adepts taking on other bodies in the yogic lore. Let us say there is a person who is close to their spiritual destination but finds their life coming to its close. Now, an accomplished yogi is capable of moving into this person's body, releasing this person's karma totally. This means you dissolve them, liberate them. Now the yogi can inhabit this body for a while, finish their own karma, and then dissolve.

It must be remembered that for the enlightened being, karma is no more a source of bondage. Right now, I have no karmic bondage at all. If I wanted to leave the body today, I could. But in order to finish some things I have started, I create a conscious karma for myself. Without some karma, the body cannot exist. So conscious karma has to be created to keep a connection to the body. Otherwise, one would be unable to retain this body.

Karma and the Courtesan's Jewelry

SUTRA #17

Those who long to leave a footprint shall never fly.

I have often spoken of the traditional courtesans in India who wore an extremely elaborate type of jewelry. Their entire body was swathed in gold and diamonds. The jewelry was so complex that the men who came to them, fired with lust, had no idea of how to take it off. It was such a dense web of chains that, although they tried hard, they could never get the jewelry off.

The ritual was a complex one. The courtesan would encourage the man to have a drink, and then another, and then yet another. He would keep drinking and trying to undo her jewelry. But he grew more and more inept, until he finally fell asleep. This is exactly what she wanted!

What he never guessed was that there was just one pin that kept the whole web of chains together. It was located in a spot that only she knew. If that single pin was pulled, the entire jewelry would fall off. Only she knew that.

Karma is exactly like this.

It is a complex web of chains—some beautiful and studded with exquisite diamonds, some of it just ugly rusted iron shackles. It makes no sense to try to pick the good karma from the bad. This is why spiritual seekers are not interested in acquiring good karma. They just want to drop the entire mess. This means burning up their karma through intense action as well as distancing themselves from it through meditation.

But there is a third way, too.

And this entails knowing the location of the elusive pin. Like the courtesans, if seekers knew where the pin was, they could find their way out of the labyrinth in just a moment. But most spend a lifetime getting more and more entangled in the karmic chains.

Where does this single pin lie?

In eliminating a single question from your life: *What about me?*

If you are able to completely eliminate this question, you have annihilated the enormous sense of self-significance that most human beings live with. Now you can dismantle the elaborate karmic chains in one swift single stroke. You emerge from the debris of your karma a liberated being.

It is because most people cannot eradicate this question that a guru was considered necessary. A guru's role has always been this: to step in to pull the pin for you when the time is right.

"So, Sadhguru, when are you going to pull my pin?" I can already envisage that question coming at me from several quarters! So let me add a caveat right away. If you ask this question, it means you are not ready yet to have your pin pulled. If you are in a state where you think your karma is a burden that must be eliminated, you are not yet ready for liberation. Only when you learn to transform every memory—conscious/unconscious, pleasant/unpleasant, beautiful/horrendous—into joy and well-being are you ready.

If you ask for the pin to be pulled when you are not ready, it is not liberation; it is escapism. There is a difference between walking out of the body and committing suicide. Suicide means you want to escape a difficult situation. Walking out of something means your term is over and you are stepping out joyfully. If you escape from prison, you will be on the run for the rest of your life. But if you are freed from prison because your term is up, you are a free man. That is the difference. And it is a big one.

In ancient times, people set sail for distant lands that they imagined were at the other end of the earth. It is only later that they realized the earth was round and that they were only going round in circles.

Traveling the globe can be wonderfully exciting. But at a certain point, one tires of going round in circles. The scenery changes, the weather alters, but there is something deep within a human being that dislikes going in circles. This innate dislike is bound to surface at some time.

The aim of this book is to remind you that *there is a way out of circles of repetitiveness.* There are many ways to walk the path of karma yoga—to become a spiritual practitioner capable of walking out of circles into an eternal and imperishable nowness. Some circles can be instantly erased. Some need some more work. Others need some extra outside help. But it is important to do all that you can. The guru—whether in a physical form or not—finally steps in to do whatever remains to be done.

The reason why human beings keep generating karma is that they want to leave a footprint. They are seeking some continuation of their individual identity. Whether it is in terms of personal achievements, relationships, bearing children, or engaging in social causes, they want desperately to leave a dent on existence, attain immortality, live on for posterity.

But those who long to leave a footprint shall never fly.

The longing to fly is deeply human. The thirst for freedom is not something that the sages invented. It is something far more primal: the longing of life for itself.

But in order to fly you need to be willing to drop all investments. You need to reach the point where you are no longer interested in saving yourself. You no longer want to take incremental steps toward your liberation. You realize that if you take incremental steps to infinity, you become endless installments and never get there. When you see your limited identity for what it really is—a hollow bundle of thoughts, likes, dislikes, and prejudices—you are ready to abandon it.

With abandon, all the shackles fall away. The final pin is unlocked. Once you take wing, webs and chains and labyrinths have no hold upon you. The roughness of the terrain, the bumpiness of the ride, is inconsequential. Suddenly you are no longer navigating your way through the din and the confusion of crazy road traffic. You are a being of the skies. You now plunge into a place that you always inhabited but were too distracted to notice. You fall headlong into *this moment*—this moment in all its radiance and power, majesty and profundity.

Do not think of karma in terms of lifetimes. Think of it in terms of just this Living Moment.

◆

. . . A day is but a piece of time
That lets us live and die.
. . . This day let us live and
Live totally.

—SADHGURU

GLOSSARY

Accumulated Karma	*See* sanchita karma.
Actionable Karma in the Future	*See* agami karma.
Actionable Karma in the Present	*See* kriyamana karma.
Adiyogi	The first yogi, one of the many epithets of Shiva.
agami karma	Actionable Karma in the Future. Inevitable consequences of present-day action that compel external action tomorrow.
akasha	Refers to the sky or ether. One of the five elements of Nature.
Akashi Mudra	A simple practice to access the element of akasha within you and enhance your perception.

Allotted Karma	*See* prarabdha karma.
ananda	Bliss.
anandamayakosha	The innermost body or the bliss body.
annamayakosha	Food-formed sheath or the gross body. One of the five sheaths of the human body in yogic physiology.
articulate memory	Impact of all the conscious information that every human being carries within.
asana	Lit. physical posture. Generally referring to yoga postures, or postures that lead one's energies to liberation. One of the eight limbs of yoga.
ashtanga yoga	The eight limbs or disciplines of yoga: yama, niyama, asana, pranayama, pratyahara, dharana, dhyana, and samadhi, as described by sage Patanjali.
atma	Sanskrit word for soul.
atomic memory	The fluctuating patterns in which the atoms function.
aum	The primordial sound made by chanting the sounds A-U-M.
avadhutas	Childlike mystics who have dropped their limited identifications so completely that they are unable to function in the outside world.

Ayurveda	Ancient Indian system of medicine.
Bhagavad Gita	One of the most sacred teachings of the Hindus. This central episode of the epic *Mahabharata* is a dialogue between Krishna and his chief disciple, Arjuna, on the battlefields of Kurukshetra. Krishna imparts to the warrior-prince Arjuna his knowledge on yoga, asceticism, dharma, and the manifold spiritual path.
bhakti	Devotion.
bhuta shuddhi	Fundamental yogic practice of cleansing the five elements that make up the human system.
bhuta shuddhi vivaha	An ancient form of consecration for marriages, originating from the yogic system, in which the couple can experience a union on the elemental level.
brahmachari	*Brahman* means divine, and *charya* means path. One who is on the path of the divine. Usually refers to one who has formally been initiated into monkhood through a certain energy process; an ascetic.
Buddha	One who is above his buddhi (intellect). Generally used to refer to Gautama the Buddha.

chakra	Lit. wheel. Also refers to the junctions of energy channels in the pranic (energy) body. Though seven major chakras are associated with the human body, there is a total of one hundred and fourteen chakras in the human system.
chitta	Dimension of intelligence unsullied by memory.
chitta vritti nirodha	Cessation of the modification of the mind, which establishes one in a state of yoga. Refers to one of the sutras by the great sage Patanjali, the father of modern yoga, in his *Yoga Sutras*.
Coimbatore	Closest major city to Isha Yoga Center, in Tamil Nadu, a state in southern India.
dharana	Maintaining mental focus. Sixth of the eight limbs of yoga.
dhi	Refers to the intellect.
dhyana	Meditative state. Seventh of the eight limbs of yoga.
Dhyanalinga	A powerful energy form at Isha Yoga Center in India, consecrated by Sadhguru exclusively for the purpose of meditation. The Dhyanalinga's granite ellipsoidal outer form is only a scaffolding for the energy form; even if it is removed the energy dimension remains. The physical form serves, in Sadhguru's words, as "a visual connection," because it is difficult for seekers to relate to an empty space.

dukkha	Suffering.
elemental memory	The memory carried by the five elements—earth, water, fire, air, and ether—which are the building blocks of creation.
evolutionary memory	The software imprinted on one's DNA that determines one's species; i.e., what makes us human beings.
Ganga	Revered river in northern India.
Gautama the Buddha	Founder of Buddhism.
genetic memory	Shared physical and psychological characteristics passed on within families.
Gita	Lit. song. Refers to the Bhagavad Gita.
guru	Lit. dispeller of darkness. A spiritual master, a realized being who guides spiritual seekers toward liberation.
Guru Nanak	Founder of Sikhism.
gurukula	Ancient Indian system of education in which the child lives and grows up in the vicinity of their guru.
hatha yoga	Physical form of yoga involving different bodily postures (asanas) and practices. Used as both a purificatory and a preparatory step for meditation and higher dimensions of spiritual experience.

Hindu	A cultural and geographical identity of the people who have inhabited the region between the Himalayas and the Indu Sagar (Indian Ocean).
ida	One of the three major pranic (energy) channels in the human body. Located on the left side of the body, it is feminine (intuitive) in nature.
inarticulate memory	Enormous reservoir of generic and specific information accumulated over eons, of which we are not aware.
isha	Formless divine energy. Also the name chosen by Sadhguru for the foundation created to offer a spiritual possibility to the world.
Isha programs	Refers to various spiritual programs offered by Isha wherein yoga is experienced as a living science.
Isha Yoga Center	A sacred space for self-transformation established by Sadhguru at the foothills of the Velliangiri Mountains in southern India.
Jain	One who practices Jainism.
janam janam	Hindi for "lifetime after lifetime."

karma	Refers to the volition with which one performs action. Karma is the mechanism by which relative existence maintains itself. Refers to past action: the cause of all bondage. That which binds one to the body and creates tendencies that rule one's life. Law of cause and effect.
Karma Samyama	Advanced spiritual program at Isha Yoga Center, in which layers of karma are brought to the surface to dissolve them.
karma yoga	Action performed joyfully and effortlessly, which liberates rather than imprisons.
karma yogi	One who follows the path of karma yoga.
karma-nashana	Destruction of karma.
karmas	Special rituals or practices performed for the dead by their families.
karma-vriddhi	Breeding or accumulation of karma.
karmic memory	The vast amount of impressions that shape us into distinct individuals—including our likes and dislikes, our personality.
kosha	Lit. sheath; vessel, layer.

Krishna	Divine incarnation, historically over thirty-five hundred years ago, Krishna is one of the most popular deities of the Hindu pantheon. A Yadava prince and the central character of the epic *Mahabharata*. His discourse to his chief disciple Arjuna in the form of Bhagavad Gita is considered the most sacred of Hindu scriptures.
kriya	Lit. act, rite. Refers to a certain class of yogic practices. Inward energy action.
kriya yoga	The path of using one's energies to reach one's ultimate nature.
kriyamana karma	Actionable Karma in the Present. Karma that compels outward action.
kshetra sanyas	Sanskrit term referring to a vow to never leave a certain consecrated geographical space.
kula vedana	The suffering of a family, a clan, or a community due to a collective memory.
kundalini	Lit. serpent power. Cosmic energy depicted as a snake coiled at the base of the spine (Muladhara chakra) and that eventually, through the practice of yoga, rises up the sushumna nadi. As it rises, the kundalini awakens each successive chakra until it reaches the Sahasrar. The manifested kundalini becomes Kula, the all-transcending light of consciousness.

linga	Lit. the first form, the primordial form. An energy form consecrated for worship, generally associated with Shiva.
Linga Bhairavi	An energized physical form, consecrated by Sadhguru, considered to be a fierce and fiery manifestation of the Divine Feminine.
Mahabharata	Historic Indian epic poem, one of the two major epics of ancient India; the longest epic poem known.
mahasamadhi	Complete dissolution of the self, also known as nirvana and mahaparinibbana in other spiritual traditions. The dropping of the physical body in full awareness.
Mahavira	Considered the founder of the Jain religion in the fifth century BC. A contemporary of Gautama the Buddha.
manomayakosha	The mental body. One of the five sheaths of the human body in yogic physiology.
Markandeya	Ancient Hindu sage who sought divine grace to triumph over death and was thus blessed to remain sixteen forever. His story stands testimony to the transformative power of human responsibility: he learned how to become available to grace and thereby transformed his destiny.

mukti	Release, liberation, final absolution of the self from the chain of death and rebirth. The highest goal of all spiritual seekers.
Mysore	City in southern India where Sadhguru was born and grew up.
namaskar	Traditional Hindu salutation that acknowledges the divinity within a person.
niyama	The second limb of yoga, used along with yama to codify the dos and don'ts of yoga.
niyoga	Ancient practice in which a king allowed his queen to bear the child of a sage to ensure a better ruler for the people.
paramatma	The divine.
Pindaris	A bandit tribe that conducted raids in central India from the 17th to 19th centuries; finally defeated by an army led by the British.
pingala	One of the three major pranic (energy) channels of the body. Located on the right side of the body. Masculine in nature.
pranamayakosha	The energy sheath, or pranic body. One of the five sheaths of yogic physiology.

pranayama	A powerful yogic practice that uses certain breathing techniques to generate and direct the flow of prana (energy) in the human body. The fourth of the eight limbs of yoga.
pranic body	Energy body. *See also* pranamayakosha.
prarabdha karma	Allotted Karma. The karma allotted for one's present life.
pratyahara	Turning inward. The fifth limb of yoga.
Ramakrishna Paramahamsa	A mid-nineteenth-century spiritual master who lived mostly in Kolkata. A devotee of the goddess Kali, he frequently went into ecstatic states of samadhi. One of his best-known disciples is Swami Vivekananda, who established and propagated the Ramakrishna Order, which today has a worldwide following.
Ramana Maharshi	Early twentieth-century spiritual master who lived in the hills of Tiruvannamalai near Chennai in southern India. His teachings revolve around self-inquiry. He is believed to have enlightened not only humans, but also a cow and a crow.
runanubandha	Physical memory of the body. The bondage caused by physical relationships.

sadhana	Lit. tool or device. Spiritual practices used as a means to self-realization.
Sadhguru	A spiritual teacher who is enlightened, or has realized the Self, whose knowledge or realization comes from within rather than any teachings learned from outside.
Sadhguru Sri Brahma	Last lifetime of Sadhguru.
sama	Equanimous.
samadhi	Deep state of equanimity, the last of the eight limbs of yoga. Greatly celebrated in the lore, experience of samadhi is immensely therapeutic and deeply transformative in nature.
samsara	The world, the existence, the domain of karma. Protracted delusion of the mind. The cycle of birth, death, and rebirth.
samskara	Ritual, in the general sense. Denotes rites such as the birth ceremony, tonsure, marriage, cremation, etc. In yoga, it stands for the indelible imprints in the subconscious left behind by daily experiences.

Samyama	A confluence of the states of dharana, dhyana, and samadhi. Here, referring to the eight-day meditation program conducted by Sadhguru in which one is transported into explosive states of meditativeness. This program is a possibility to shed lifetimes of karma and experience samadhi.
sanchita karma	Accumulated Karma. Karma that has been accumulated over lifetimes.
sankara	Reaction; the fourth aspect of the mind as defined by Gautama the Buddha.
sanya	Recognition; the second aspect of the mind as defined by Gautama the Buddha.
sensory memory	The impact our physical and cultural environments have on our system, the way our body and mind respond to the world.
shakti	Lit. power, energy. The active aspect of emptiness. The creation is envisioned as a play of Shiva and Shakti, which symbolizes the duality of existence or the yin and yang.
Shambhavi Mahamudra	A 21-minute yogic practice taught by Sadhguru that balances and activates one's energy system, conferring both physiological and psychological benefits.

Shankaran Pillai	The hero in many of Sadhguru's jokes and anecdotes. He is usually a frail man whose idiocies are typical of the common man.
Shiva	Lit. that which is not. The Great Lord. The destroyer in the trinity.
Siddha	Ancient Indian system of medicine.
siddhi	Power, paranormal or supernormal accomplishment.
Sohni and Mahiwal	Lovers in a tragic Indian love story.
swayambhu	Self-created.
teertha	Consecrated water; here referring to consecrated spaces.
vasanas	Lit. smell. Tendencies or desire; subliminal trait left behind in the mind by action and desire.
vedana	Sensation; the third aspect of the mind as defined by Gautama the Buddha.
Velayudhampalayam	Village in the state of Tamil Nadu, India.
vignanamayakosha	The etheric body. One of the five sheaths of the human body in yogic physiology.

vinyana	Cognition; the first aspect of the mind as defined by Gautama the Buddha.
yagna	Sacrifice; one of the main pillars of the Vedic ritual system.
yagna bhoomi	Land of sacrifice, where yagnas are performed.
yama	The first limb of yoga, used along with niyama to codify the dos and don'ts of yoga.
yoga	Lit. union.
yogi	One who is in a state of yoga.
Zen	A Buddhist spiritual tradition. The Japanese word *zen* is derived from the Chinese word *chan*, which in turn is a transliteration of the Sanskrit word *dhyana*, meaning meditation.

Ranked among the fifty most influential people in India, Sadhguru is a yogi, mystic, and visionary. He has been conferred three presidential awards in India, including one for his environmental work as well as the country's highest annual civilian award for exceptional and distinguished service.

Sadhguru is a speaker and opinion-maker of international renown. He has spoken at various forums across the world, including the United Nations, the World Economic Forum, the World Bank, the UK House of Lords, TED, and Microsoft and Google headquarters. He has also been invited to speak at leading educational institutions—Oxford, Stanford, Harvard, Yale, Wharton, and MIT, among others.

Over the years, Sadhguru has launched large ecological initiatives. The movements Rally for Rivers and Cauvery Calling address the urgent need to revitalize Indian rivers and issues related to soil, water, and climate change. Recognized globally for their wide reach and impact, these initiatives have become game-changers by establishing a global blueprint for economic development that is ecologically sustainable. Sadhguru has been invited by global agencies such as UNEP (United Nations Environment Programme), UNCCD (United Nations Convention to Combat Desertification), IUCN (International Union for Conservation of Nature), and others to discuss global solutions to the world's ecological issues.

Sadhguru's celebratory engagement with life includes an active involvement in fields as diverse as architecture, visual design, poetry, painting, sports, music, aviation, and motorcycling.

Three decades ago, Sadhguru founded Isha Foundation, a nonprofit human-service organization, with human well-being as its core commitment. The foundation has initiated powerful yoga programs for human transformation and path-breaking outreach projects to uplift rural communities. Isha is supported by over 11 million volunteers in more than 300 centers worldwide.

Also by

SADHGURU

Available wherever books are sold

HARMONY
BOOKS · NEW YORK